# Helicopters: The British Columbia Story

# Helicopters: The British Columbia Story

*Peter Corley-Smith and David N. Parker*

*Colour profile illustrations by Clive Brooks*

CANAV Books

Published in association with the
British Columbia Provincial Museum, Victoria, B.C.

Published by
CANAV Books
Larry Milberry, Publisher
51 Balsam Avenue
Toronto M4E 3B6
Canada

**Canadian Cataloguing in Publication Data**
Corley-Smith, Peter, 1923–
  Helicopters: the British Columbia story

Includes index.
Bibliography: p.
ISBN 0-9690703-5-7.

1. Helicopter transportation–British Columbia –History. 2. Helicopters–History. I. Parker, David. II. Title.

HE9793.C22B72 1985      387.7'3352'09711
C85-098514-5

TYPESETTING
Arlene and Eva Weber, Second Story Graphics

PHOTO RETOUCHING
Stephen Ng, SNG Retouching Studio

REPRO ASSEMBLY
Rob Devine and Betty Mason, Printart

PROOFREADING
Ralph Clint

Printed and bound in Canada by the Bryant Press Limited, Toronto

*(Facing title page) Quasar Helicopters' Bell 214ST at Abbotsford, August 11, 1982. (Ken Swartz)*

*(Title page) Canada's first Sikorsky S-55, operated by Okanagan for Alcan on the Kitimat project in northern B.C. (Morrison Knudsen Co.)*

*(Opposite) A Bell 204 perched in a B.C. alpine meadow. (Alpine Helicopters)*

*(Below) An Alouette II turbine helicopter in use in British Columbia. (R.D. Turner)*

# Contents

*The colour profile paintings appear between pages 48 and 49.*

*The early days. Okanagan's first helicopter,
CF-FZX, shows all its 1946 charm. (via Jack
McNulty)*

# Foreword

*Alf Stringer at Victoria, 1984.*
*(D.N. Parker)*

When I first heard that this book was being prepared, I was, for a number of reasons, delighted. First, I knew that if the British Columbia Provincial Museum had a hand in it, the results were bound to be more than satisfactory. Second, I knew that Larry Milberry publishes the most attractive and comprehensive aviation books in Canada. And third, I knew that the authors weren't outsiders, writing with superficial knowledge of the subject. One was an aviation historian with a growing interest in helicopters, the other a writer with 20 years experience as a commercial helicopter pilot.

Now that I have seen the finished manuscript, I know too that my confidence was justified. While this book does not attempt to provide a definitive history of helicopter flying in British Columbia, it does trace the most important developments, in both the private and the public sectors; and it does so mostly in the words of the people who took part in these developments, both the pioneers and those currently active. The result is to bring to life the trials and errors, the failures and the successes—and the sheer fun of doing something entirely new—in a way that formal history seldom can.

And finally, from my point of view, it is gratifying to see any book about helicopters in Canada. For some reason aviation historians have chosen to ignore this subject. They seem to feel that helicopters are not really part of the aviation scene. I am sure this book will at least make a dent in that curious prejudice—just as I am sure that anyone in the aviation business will enjoy reading it.

Alf Stringer

# Preface

We begin by emphasizing that this book does not presume to be a definitive history of the helicopter in British Columbia; we had neither the time nor the resources to embark on such an ambitious venture. Instead, we have brought together the story of helicopter flying as recalled by some of the participants—people who were clearly pioneers in a new technology.

In fact, the history of helicopter operations in British Columbia is comparatively brief, extending over a mere 35 years, or slightly less than half that of fixed-wing aircraft in this province. Perhaps for this reason, published sources are few in number. According to a computer search, and to the best of our knowledge, only one book on helicopter flying per se has been published in Canada. Much reliance, therefore, has been placed on the recollections of those actually involved in events described, and these have later been corroborated and in some instances, expanded upon, when personal records such as logbooks or similar primary accounts were consulted as part of the review process.

Other sources we have investigated include company annual reports, reports of government agencies, trade-journal and newspaper articles. These have often been useful in establishing or confirming a chronology of events and technological developments and their significance. They have also provided clues to further contacts or information. Additionally, we have been given access to a considerable body of primary source material.

Interviews were conducted to bring out certain information and then were fully transcribed. Excerpts chosen for inclusion were carefully edited. This process involved the removal of interviewers' questions, normal repetitiveness in conversation, and speech habits that would have made the translation from transcript to prose difficult. Each person interviewed read, and approved, the appropriate excerpts.

Personal experience has inevitably provided the basis for the "Life in the Bush" chapters; to have written from secondary sources would probably have reduced this side of the story, a central aspect of it, to rather uninteresting descriptive prose that would have lost the intimacy desired.

In preparing this book, the authors needed a great deal of assistance. Fortunately it was always available.

Our most valuable help in the area of commercial flying came from A.H. "Barney" Bent, one of the original partners in Okanagan Air Services and, until the summer of 1982, a member of the board of directors of Okanagan Helicopters Limited. Barney Bent had prepared a manuscript on the history of the company; in his generosity, he allowed us full access to that document and to the files of the company.

We must also thank Cherry Graf of Okanagan Helicopters, who was always able to find exactly the document or photograph we needed. Both she and Barney spent considerable time reviewing material for us, as did Walter Palubski, Don MacKenzie and Ken Blackwood. Ken has been our liaison through much of this project.

Alf Stringer, president of Vancouver Island Helicopters, contributed a great deal of his time helping us to assemble information on the early days of both the Okanagan and Vancouver Island companies, as did his wife Lynn. Alf and Eric Cowden preserved us, we hope to a large extent, from technical errors, particularly in the evolution of the Bell 47 series of helicopters.

Lieutenant-Colonel Gordon Diamond, former Commanding Officer of 442 Squadron, Canadian Armed Forces, outlined the operation of the Search and Rescue facilities on the West Coast and reviewed the SAR chapter for accuracy. Ensign Jeff Vail, Lieutenant-Commander Dennis Maclean and Commander Paul Milligan of the United States Coast Guard gave us access to their records and reviewed out material, while Lieutenant Richard Wall, United States Navy, provided material about the Perfect Pass crash.

Bob Jones and Ian Duncan of the Canadian Coast Guard were very helpful in providing photographic material of Coast Guard operations. Bob made several important suggestions for additions to the manuscript.

Harvey H. Lippincott and Bob Carroll of United Technologies supplied information and photographs relating to the development of Sikorsky helicopters and their operation by Okanagan Helicopters in British Columbia.

Members of various British Columbia Ministries provided considerable assistance: Helmut Braditsch, Jack McClelland and Hugh Lyons in Forestry provided the bulk of material on inventory/valuation techniques and read the manuscript for accuracy; Peter Robbin and the staff at the Forestry photo lab spent time with us to ferret out suitable photographic material; Don Pearson of Environment provided photographic material and assisted in verifying British Columbia place names.

Within our own institution, we are grateful for the approval and support of R. Yorke Edwards, our Director. Our friend and colleague, Bob Turner, Industrial History Curator, read the manuscript at every stage and insisted, as he does with his own writing, on the removal of clichés and circumlocutions. Don Gallacher, Curator of Modern History read the manuscript and offered advice and support. Terry Hanna spent many hours typing from virtually indecipherable copy without complaint. Harold Hosford, Museum Publications Editor, has helped us carry the project to this stage, and Doug Lockhart, our administrator, made it possible to get transcripts of all the interviews we conducted.

Dr. Paul Spitzer, Corporate Historian for the Boeing Company in Seattle, evaluated sections of the book and made suggestions which have resulted in improvements. Bob Bradford, Curator of the National Aviation Museum in Ottawa,also read the manuscript.

Inevitably it has been necessary to borrow material used in other publications and the support of the following publishers is sincerely appreciated: *Scientific American,* New York; William Heinemann Ltd., London; Paris; Dodd, Mead and Company, New York; Macdonald's, London; *Approach,* Norfolk, Va.; J.B. Lippincott Ltd., New York; Max Parrish, London.

Other institutions have allowed us to use photographic material: the Victoria *Times-Colonist*; Visual Records Section, Provincial Archives of British Columbia; Public Archives of Canada, Ottawa; United States Coast Guard; United States Navy; Canadian Armed Forces; Vancouver *Province*; Vancouver Public Library; and the Victoria City Archives.

Cartography students of Camosun College, Victoria, produced the map used in the book, and their instructors, Ron Deakin and Bill Sinclair, never hesitated in seeing that requested information was added. We're grateful for their support.

Peter Corley-Smith
David N. Parker

# Introduction

Helicopters were the answer to the problems of flying in British Columbia's mountains. Few realized this at first, not even the original crew working in the Okanagan Valley in 1947. But the province's great mountain barriers, which for so long had obstructed travel, construction and exploration, were where the helicopter's unique potential would be realized.

Months after the first commercial certification had been granted to a helicopter manufacturer in North America, a small company began agricultural spraying with a helicopter in British Columbia. This venture was not a success, but another the following year, this time on forests rather than orchards, convinced the company that the opportunity for commercial success lay in flying the mountains—in providing quick access to the vast interior of British Columbia, dominated by range after range of previously inaccessible mountains.

The opportunities and needs were certainly there—access for mapping, mineral exploration, forestry, search and rescue, and construction—but a whole range of flying techniques had to be developed and perfected. It was a dangerous, nerve-testing period for the pilots but it was also a great adventure. In 1947, the Royal Canadian Air Force, using Sikorsky H-5s, began operations in a search and rescue capacity and commercial operations were becoming established. By the late '50s helicopters had proved their worth beyond question and were in use throughout the province. By the early '60s the Canadian Coast Guard began using them to supply and service lighthouses and other marine navigational aids, and to serve as pathfinders for the icebreakers in the Arctic during the summer months. In 1973, the Royal Canadian Mounted Police began flying helicopters.

But it was the commercial crews which led the way and, because of this, while attempting to do justice to all the organizations flying helicopters in the early days, it was inevitable that this book became in large part the story of one company: Okanagan Helicopters Limited. It was the Okanagan crews which first tackled and finally solved the problems of mountain flying. It was to them that the military and other government departments went to learn this new art. In short, Okanagan's crews established a second bush flying era.

Bush flying got its start in the 1920s when legendary pilots like Punch Dickins, Doc Oaks, Wop May, and Walter Gilbert were opening up the North to more than the missionaries and Hudson's Bay traders. Accompanied by their engineers, people like Pete Darbyshire, Bill Nadin, Alex Milne, Stan Knight and Al Cheesman, their sleeping bags and some emergency rations in the back, they set off, often with no maps, to explore the country in machines which were still balky and temperamental. They had to feel their way as they went; and to learn, of course, they had to make mistakes. They had to find out by experience what a reasonable ice or snow surface for a landing looked like from the air. They had to discover the hard way what happened when they tried to land on glassy water without instruments. They had to learn to read the wind and the waves on the lakes, the furrows on the snow, the dull, opaque appearance of soft ice. And with a bit of luck and enough skill and resourcefulness, they would survive to profit from their mistakes and pass on their knowledge to others. Much the same thing happened when helicopters made their appearance in the Canadian bush.

Those involved in this second wave of bush flying were like their predecessors, people of strong character. In British Columbia for the first 10 years, nearly all of them worked for the same two companies: Okanagan Air Services (which became Okanagan Helicopters in 1952) and Vancouver Island Helicopters. The very first crew was Carl Agar (pilot) and Alf Stringer (engineer). They were soon training others: pilots Bill McLeod, Deke Orr, Fred Snell, Peter Cornwall, Ted Henson and Bob Taylor; engineers Jock Graham, Sig Hubenig, Bill Smith, Gordy Askin, Eric Cowden and Art Johnson.

These were self-reliant, resourceful and courageous people. They had to be, for they were doing something no one else had done. They had to learn to estimate the wind and turbulence on high mountain ridges, or judge from the air the firmness of a swamp in a forest clearing. They had to try out new techniques, hoping their experiments would not prove fatal. They were working in remote areas, affected by the tensions which small groups living close together are bound to experience. It was a hard life and, in the early days particularly, the financial rewards were slight.

Fortunately there were compensations. Time and familiarity have made us indifferent now, but in the late 1940s and early 1950s there was still a touch of magic about the helicopter—the same sort of feeling people experienced when Paul McCready's *Gossamer Albatross* was pedalled across the English Channel by the young Californian, Bryan Allen. The frontiers of flight have always captured the imagination.

And because of this, when a helicopter landed anywhere at that time, and there were people about, they would come running to look at it; to take photographs, tap the plastic bubble, and marvel at its flimsiness. It was heady stuff. Helicopter crews had become people of some distinction—successful, and with a sort of pleasant self-confidence which had nothing to do with arrogance.

In our research for this book, we interviewed not only helicopter crews, but some of the people who first employed them in what sometimes seemed like the combat zone of bush and mountain flying. Employers spoke with respect of the intelligence and all-round competence of their helicopter crews. To give just one example, Ernie McMinn, of the

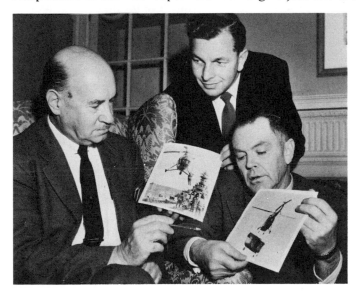

*Igor Sikorsky, Alf Stringer and Carl Agar discuss helicopters at a Vancouver hotel in 1954. Sikorsky and Agar were close friends by then. (United Technologies/ Sikorsky Aircraft)*

Provincial Topographic Surveys: ''This was one of the great things about Okanagan: the kind of guys they had were top rate; they were interested, and got to know the requirements of the job within a short time, and they could just about do it.''

The early fixed-wing bush pilots of the '20s and '30s had a similar rapport with their customers. But in helicopters this closeness was emphasized. Whereas the fixed-wing pilots were usually engaged in supply and transport, the helicopter pilots became an integral part of the job. They took surveyors out on the line and sometimes worked with them as rod-men or helped cut line for theodolite sightings. They became knowledgeable about geology—though not very often, as far as we know, when it came to stock exchange transactions. They learned about oil exploration techniques, and came to know much about our forests and how they were managed.

It was this personal involvement, so different from the concept of an airborne taxi driver, that made helicopter crews an interesting and vital part of British Columbia's history. While the pilot was devising new ways of accelerating progress on a job, the engineer would often be working to improve living conditions in camp—constructing a shower with 10-gallon drum propped in the trees and a perforated plastic bottle for a shower head; or repairing a balky electric generator; or working on the camp's two-way radio, which broke down more often than a teenager's jalopy.

However, to convey the impression that life in a bush camp was an image of harmony would be misleading. Just as the helicopter crews were individualistic, so also were the surveyors, geologists and foresters. And in the confinement and isolation of a bush camp, personality clashes were the rule rather than the exception.

For the pilot, the qualities of a helicopter gave him a sense of power—he could vault over a tall building, or a mountain for that matter. He was in many ways the centre of the operation. Without him nothing much could be accomplished, and it required a strong character indeed to withstand the temptation to try usurping the party chief's authority.

With the engineer, on the other hand, a different problem emerged. He had to work in the evening, very often when the mosquitos and blackflies were at their worst. While the rest of the camp were relaxing, talking about what they had done and seen during the day—enjoying what small social life there is in a bush camp—the engineer was out on his lonely job, greasing, cleaning, fixing the mechanical snags the pilot had reported.

During the day, he stayed in camp with the cook. At first, those ingenious and productive things he did to improve living conditions were much appreciated. But as time wore on, they began to be taken for granted. Worse yet, he began to be looked upon as a sort of handy man, expected to gather wood for the stoves, carry water for the cook— there were any number of things that might be expected of him as he waited all day with little to do. Some handled this sort of thing tactfully, others with growing resentment. In either case, it was all part of the dynamics of life in a helicopter operation bush camp.

Meanwhile, there was a question of progress. The advantages of improved technology are not always immediately apparent, and this is evident in the development of helicopters. The first Bell machines—the 47-B3, 47-D and 47-G—were equipped with wooden blades, which were inclined to soak up moisture, altering their delicate balance and causing vibrations. As well, they were fragile, tending to split even if they struck a willow no thicker than one's little finger, or break off altogether if they hit anything more substantial.

Then came metal blades which could cut through the tops of small trees without being damaged. But this led to a new problem. If the tree tops were thick enough, or the object happened to be a rock instead of a tree, the blade didn't break; instead the whole helicopter would be hurled in the opposite direction to the path of the blade—usually to the detriment of both the helicopter and the pilot.

Similarly, the first Bells performed marginally in the mountains. Pilots yearned for more power, for the superchargers with which so many fixed-wing aircraft engines were equipped. The advent of the helicopter turbocharger in the late '50s, which maintained sea-level power up to 10,000 feet, took much of the terror out of mountain flying. As always, though, there was a penalty. If one did have an accident, fuel nearly always spilled onto the red-hot turbocharger and the machine would catch fire.

The next development was the turbine engine. This, it was claimed, would bring significant advantages: the power-to-weight ratio was a big improvement over the conventional piston engine; maintenance would be minimal, performance and reliability remarkable.

The first claim was incontestable, the second two something of a joke to begin with. One unfortunate pilot set off across Canada on a demonstration flight with a light turbine helicopter. He experienced four engine failures. The last one, which occurred while he was flying through the Rogers Pass in British Columbia, earned him some grey hairs. He lined up for a forced landing on a pull-off viewpoint beside the highway. Just as he settled into his final approach, a camper drove into the parking area and stopped for its occupants to admire the view. The pilot managed to slip over the edge of the viewpoint and go on down for a landing on the rocky bank of the Illecillewaet River. He was a professional. He managed to put down with little damage to the helicopter.

The results of this disparity between promise and reality were interesting. When the first light turbines—the Bell 206, the Hiller 1100 and, a little later, the Hughes 500—began to appear in commercial flying, they were all flown by senior pilots. A year and many flame-outs and forced landings later, the senior pilots were all back in piston-engined machines; the turbines were being flown by the "young turks." Some time passed before the grizzled veterans would climb back into the turbines. They were wise, because it turned out that the unreliability lasted for some time and, in the case of one model, there was a fundamental defect which resulted in its disappearance from the British Columbia scene for some years.

Since both the Canadian Coast Guard and the RCMP first operated helicopters somewhat beyond our definition of the early days, coverage of their operations is limited. This does not imply a hierarchy of importance: both these organizations have provided valuable service to the province, but they were not among the pioneers of helicopter flying in British Columbia.

There is one factor, however, that should be mentioned: a misunderstanding with the Canadian Coast Guard. The name suggests to the general public a search and rescue role, and they are frequently criticized in the media for failing to fulfill this function. But in the late 1940s the federal government decided that the armed forces would deal with rescue and the Coast Guard with supply and maintenance of marine navigational aids. It would cost vast sums of money now to reorganize and re-equip the Coast Guard for SAR duties; and in any case, they would merely be duplicating the excellent organization provided by the armed forces.

As for the Search and Rescue services provided by the RCAF and, more recently, the Canadian Forces, theirs is a story which deserves a book of its own. Within the limits of our resources, we only hope that we have done these government services at least a measure of justice.

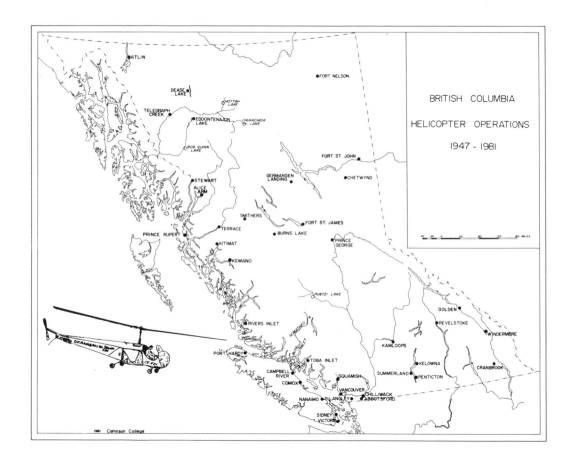

BRITISH COLUMBIA

HELICOPTER OPERATIONS

1947 - 1981

# Okanagan Air Services Limited: A Trip to Yakima

*And that's how it started: through Carl and Barney Bent
and some of the others sitting in a coffee shop in Penticton
and reading this magazine.*

ALF STRINGER

The history of the helicopter goes back all the way to such distinguished minds as Archimedes and Leonardo da Vinci. Da Vinci, using principles proposed by Archimedes some 700 years earlier produced a design for a "helix" which appeared in a 1505 manuscript. But this was theoretical, and as it turned out, the aerodynamics and engineering involved in the production of a helicopter were so complex that another 400 years of experimentation—of trial and error, often comic, sometimes tragic—were to pass before the first practical examples of the concept took to the air more or less simultaneously in Europe and the United States in the late 1930s.

In British Columbia, the first commercial helicopter flight took place only a decade later, in August 1947, over the fruit orchards of Penticton and Summerland in the Okanagan Valley. Although it aroused some interest and excitement among the local population, few at the time seem to have realized what an impact this new machine would have on the future of the province.

The principals in this pioneering venture, Carl Agar, Alf Stringer and Barney Bent, were all ex-RCAF and struggling to stay in aviation after the Second World War. Carl and Barney were both pilots; they had served together as flying instructors at Abbotsford in the Fraser Valley. Alf Stringer had served with them as a maintenance engineer.

All three were discharged from the RCAF as soon as the war ended. As with many others, Agar and Bent, together with another ex-RCAF pilot, Andy Duncan, began their civilian careers in aviation trying to run a flying club, in this case in Penticton. One of the first needs was to find a competent maintenance engineer to look after their machines, and Agar travelled to Vancouver to persuade Alf Stringer, then working as a garage mechanic in the lower mainland, to join them. Alf didn't really regard it as a golden opportunity. He recalls that "Carl Agar came down to Vancouver; he spent some time talking to me and decided, I guess when he went back to the people who were going to form this club, that I'd be a likely subject to tighten the nuts and bolts for them. They decided to hire me and I headed up to the Okanagan Valley. The deal in Penticton didn't sound too awe-inspiring but there wasn't much going on in aviation at that time anyway, so I thought I'd give it a whirl."

And business was slow. Few people at the time could afford to fly for pleasure and there was a surplus of ex-service pilots ready to fill any jobs which did become available. So the new partners soon decided to branch out into the charter business. They set up as Okanagan Air Services Ltd. and began to investigate what seemed the most likely road to success: aerial spraying. The Okanagan Valley is the prime fruit growing area in the

*This closed cockpit Bell 47-B3 was in use in Yakima when Carl Brady trained Carl Agar in 1947. (Carl Brady)*

province, producing apples, pears, peaches, apricots, cherries, plums and grapes, all of which need spraying to protect them from insects in the summer season.

If aerial spraying seemed an obvious commercial possibility, a look at spray operators over the border in the Wenatchee district of Washington state tended to be discouraging. "We were shocked at the mortality rate of their pilots and aircraft," Barney Bent recalls. "We looked around at one another; there was Carl Agar and myself as pilots and Alf Stringer as the engineer. I think it was Alf who summed it up. 'Well,' he said, 'we could last at least six months with you two.'"

Alf Stringer describes the next move: "In 1946 Carl and a couple of the people who were involved with the flying club were sitting in the coffee shop in Penticton. I guess Carl had picked up the mail and read in one of the aviation magazines that a company called Central Aircraft, which operated from Yakima in Washington and had been in the aerial spray business for years, was going to go into helicopters because they looked like the answer for spraying. [The principal advantages were slow speed and remarkable manoeuvrability, and the fact that the downwash from the rotor blades drove the insecticide down into the foliage of the plants below.]

"We were thinking of equipping one of our Tiger Moths to do spraying. So we thought, well, since we didn't know anything about spraying, we might as well start out with two unknowns. If we could get some people interested in helicopters—we knew the fruit growers were interested in spraying because their livelihoods depended on it—and get some money together, we'd get into the helicopter business. And that's how it started: through Carl and Barney Bent and some of the others sitting in a coffee shop in Penticton and reading a magazine."

Unlike Agar and Stringer, Barney Bent had other resources besides flying. His family was involved in a metal fabrication business, one of the offshoots of which manufactured ground spray equipment for the fruit growers in the Okanagan. As a consequence, he was perhaps naturally interested in the potential advantages of using helicopters for this purpose, and he agreed to a preliminary visit to evaluate the experimental helicopter operation in Yakima. He, Agar and Stringer went down together, experienced their first demonstration helicopter rides in an open-cockpit Bell 47-B3, and returned to Penticton convinced that helicopters would provide all the answers to the problems of spraying fruit orchards. As it turned out, they were wrong about the spraying, but fortunately for them the helicopter had other potential.

To continue with Alf's description: "So we went down to Yakima, where the Bell Company had a helicopter. [The Bell Company's main plant was in Buffalo, New York]. They were actually testing—they weren't even at FAA (Federal Aviation Adminstration)

*Barney Bent (left) served, with Carl Agar, as a flying instructor in the RCAF. (Below) Carl Agar and Alf Stringer with their new Bell 47-B3 after its arrival in British Columbia in July 1947. The castoring forward wheels allowed manoeuvring on the ground. This was a throwback to fixed-wing taxiing and not really needed on a helicopter, which can move slowly in any direction a foot or two above the ground. The hoppers and discharge tubes for insecticide are behind the cockpit. Agricultural models of the B3 had open cockpits. For crop dusting or spraying the B3 could fly safely at a lower altitude than fixed-wing aircraft. These were generally converted military training aircraft such as Tiger Moths. (Okanagan Helicopters Collection, Stocks Family Collection/Interior Photo Bank)*

*Carl Brady today is president and chairman of the board of Economy Rotor Aids (ERA) Helicopters, a large Alaska-based company with over 100 helicopters and 15 fixed-wing aircraft. ERA was established by Brady in Yakima in 1948 as Economy Pest Control-Economy Helicopters. (Carl Brady)*

certification yet—but they took us up for a demonstration ride. Then we got back and tried to work up some enthusiasm among the fruit growers, then formed a public company and got the helicopter business started. In the spring of 1947, I went down to Yakima and started on a maintenance engineer's course. After a while Carl came along and started on the pilot's course and we went from there.''

But while the three principals of Okanagan Air Services may have been confident that helicopters were the answer, persuading businessmen to invest was another matter—until, as is the case with many successful business ventures in their early stages, luck intervened. A group of businessmen in Penticton had decided to form a new airline to service the interior of the province. Led by Douglas Dewar, a distinguished New York chartered accountant who had retired in Penticton, and Ernie Buckerfield, owner of a large feed supply company, and O.St.P. Aitkens, Gordon Butler and James B. Kidston, they had applied to the Air Transport Board for a licence to operate. Their application was turned down in favour of Canadian Pacific Airlines.

Okanagan Air Services was quick to spot the potential. As Barney put it: ''So we said to ourselves, here's a fine opportunity: here are two or three people of substance who have obviously had their financing put together for the other airline—let's see if we can interest them. Which we did. They weren't exactly overjoyed to get into the helicopter business because they'd had their hearts set on the fixed-wing deal. But Mr. Dewar did agree to head up the company, Okanagan Air Services Limited. Even so, we had all sorts of problems raising $50,000 to buy the first helicopter. A helicopter at that time cost $35,000, plus a few spares and some training for Alf Stringer as an engineer and Carl as a pilot.''

The machine being considered was the Bell 47-B3, powered by a 178 horsepower Franklin engine. Instead of sitting horizontally as it did in fixed-wing aircraft, the engine was mounted vertically, with fuel tanks beneath, and the transmission and rotor mast above. The early models required plenty of maintenance. Grease nipples and grease boots were still in the future, so the helicopter had to be taken apart after every 25 flying hours to be greased. The transmission, too, had to be taken apart and have bearings replaced every 25 hours. The maintenance man had his hands full.

Fortunately for Alf, he was trained by an expert: Joe Beebe of Central Aircraft in Yakima had worked with Bell from early design stages during the war; thus he knew as much about the Bell 47 as any engineer. For Carl, things were different. He was trained by Carl Brady, who had only 25 hours helicopter flying time. So the two Carls were very much learning together.

*Power lines are virtually invisible to low-flying helicopters and an encounter with them will often have drastic results. Carl Agar had just such an accident in 1948 and Alf Stringer spent the following winter rebuilding the machine. Stringer seems to be removing the rotor in the second photograph. A truck-mounted A-frame was necessary when dismantling the helicopter. (Andy Duncan photos/Okanagan Helicopters Collection)*

When they actually started operating in British Columbia, everything looked promising. Dr. James Marshall, an entomologist at the Dominion Experimental Station in Summerland, gave considerable support because he was aware that the fruit growers in the Okanagan were in danger of unintentionally sterilizing their land with too much insecticide. In trying to wipe out pest insects, they had been using as much as 1000 gallons of dilute sprays to the acre. From the air, they could achieve the same effect with perhaps 5 or 6 gallons. But there were to be setbacks before they discovered this. The first operational flight took place, with insecticidal dust, over a test plot on the Wally Mutch orchard, just outside Penticton. The downwash from the rotor blades bounced off the

*M.V. Gillard (left seat) and Al Soutar at Sioux Lookout, Ontario, in July 1947. This machine was later purchased by Okanagan and used in British Columbia. (Ontario Department of Lands and Forests)*

ground, forcing the dust into the air again and the helicopter promptly disappeared from sight. Liquid spray equipment was used for the next test.

Now they discovered that their troubles were connected with the functioning of the spray equipment and the logistics involved. Alf found himself spending far more time clearing plugged-up spray nozzles than on maintaining the helicopter. And when he did manage to keep the spray equipment operating for any length of time, they made the second disconcerting discovery: that they could spray at the rate of an acre a minute.

This would have been enormously encouraging if they had been dealing with large acreages. But the orchards were small and diverse, and each required a different kind of spray mixture. Had they succeeded in solving the spray equipment problem, they would have needed a dozen helicopters all working at once to meet the demand during the relatively short season. Ironically, their very success made the operation unmanageable, for they would also have needed a large staff, equipped with a fleet of fuel and chemical tankers and other vehicles to support the helicopters. Then there would be the problem of what to do with staff and equipment when the spraying season was over.

Just as they were facing these problems, disaster struck. Carl flew into some power lines and seriously damaged the helicopter—though fortunately not himself. It was a discouraging moment for the fledgling company, but their backers apparently never wavered. As Barney recalls: "We had a quick meeting right after it happened and Mr. Dewar and Mr. Buckerfield put it to the three of us: 'Do you want to carry on or don't you?' As far as I was concerned, it was up to Carl—he was flying the thing—and there was no question in his mind: 'Get the thing fixed; let's get back at it,' he replied, and that's just what we did."

They had started work at the beginning of August with their first machine CF-FZX. Now, less than a month later, it was grounded—damaged beyond immediate repair. But there were still two or three weeks of contract spraying and they managed to lease a Bell 47-B3 helicopter, CF-FZN, from Skyways Services of Winnipeg, which had decided to open a base in Vancouver but couldn't find any work for its machine. In the fall, after their first contract with the leased machine, Alf put CF-FZX on a truck and drove it to Bell's facilities at Yakima. He spent most of the winter rebuilding it from scratch, the first of many helicopters he was to repair in the years to come.

In the spring of 1948, Okanagan learned another fact about helicopters which, in retrospect, seems obvious. While a majority of the population might suffer from natural disasters, helicopter operators almost invariably benefit from them. When floods, land-slides, avalanches or forest fires occur, the helicopter becomes invaluable. The spring of 1948 brought one of the biggest floods in the history of the lower Fraser Valley. Among the consequences was a plague of mosquitos severe enough to endanger people's health. Okanagan Air Services was awarded a government contract to spray parts of the valley. This turned out to be more practical than orchard spraying. Carl was faced with wide open fields and sloughs, and the spray consisted of a mixture of 99 percent fuel oil laced with DDT, a mixture which did not clog the jets of their equipment. The operation was a success.

Meantime, Okanagan had doubled its fleet. The machine they had leased from Sky-ways the previous summer had been returned to Winnipeg at the end of the season and it too was wrecked in an accident. Skyways ran into financial problems, was unable to rebuild the machine and went out of business. After some skirmishing with the insurance company, Okanagan took over the remains for, in Barney's words, "a dollar down and a dollar when they caught us sort of thing. The insurance company was happy to make almost any kind of deal to get it off their hands."

The spraying job in the Fraser Valley had attracted attention and publicity, and this led to another worthwhile operation—a contract with the provincial forest service to spray the Windermere Valley in the East Kootenays, where the forests were infested with the "false hemlock looper" (*Nepytia canosaria*). This operation lasted July 1–24, and again it was easy spraying; the only potential problem was that they were working between 2500 feet and 4500 feet—altitudes which even the maker of the helicopter

*During the Windermere operation in July 1948, Alf Stringer followed Carl and the B3 with a pickup truck stocked with fuel and spare parts. The spray-bars seem to be receiving attention in this photo. (British Columbia Ministry of Forests)*

*Before turbocharging, helicopters like this 47-B3 would be pushed to performance limits when operating in the mountains, particularly in hot weather. In late fall or winter, as in this photo, colder air provided greater lift. From a landing pad right on the side of a hill, the pilot could literally drop the helicopter over the side, gaining air speed and lift. (Bill McLeod)*

considered marginal for operations because, as you go higher, the air becomes less dense, the rotors provide less lift, and engine power diminishes.

But Carl Agar was more than equal to the challenge, and began to develop the mountain flying techniques for which he later became celebrated. He found that flying over mountains, landing in small clearings or on sandbars in the creeks and rivers was not only feasible but thoroughly exhilarating. And what was perhaps more important, the forest service was delighted with the results. For the first time, everyone involved began to realize the potential of the helicopter for other tasks besides spraying. People could be lifted over mountains and dropped in small clearings, perhaps even dropped on mountain tops. The future looked promising if they could make their machine do what Carl Agar felt it could do.

Carl still had much to overcome. For example, when learning to drive a car, the driver has to rehearse certain movements, thinking consciously about how to change gear —right foot off the accelerator, left foot down on the clutch, move the gear shift, left foot up, right foot down—and so on. In time, of course, this becomes a reflex. The difficulty faced by early helicopter pilots was that they had to unlearn the reflexes they had developed in flying fixed-wing aircraft, and learn a new set of reflexes. In a fixed-wing aircraft, you must maintain forward speed because it is the relative airflow, acting on the wing, that provides lift. If you let the speed drop below a certain limit, you will stall and drop out of the sky. In a helicopter, because the wing is rotating at a more or less constant speed, you do not have to worry about forward speed as a means of staying in the air, unless you are high in the mountains, where the air is thin. This was the problem Carl Agar had to solve: how to get a machine which had enough power to land in the mountains without forward speed, but not enough to take off again, back into the air.

Although the pilot does not have to worry too much about forward speed when coming in to land, in physics there are no miracles, and the helicopter pilot has another anxiety: he has to maintain rotor speed. On the early Bell helicopters, the engine had to be operated between 2900 and 3100 revolutions per minute. The rotor turned at about one-tenth of this speed—from 290 to 310 revs. The "collective" lever, which controlled this aspect of helicopter flying, lay to the left of the pilot's seat. Moving it up and down altered the pitch on the main rotors, giving more or less lift; and the twist-grip throttle on the end of the "collective" fed in more or less power to maintain the desired revs.

Another difference between the airplane and the helicopter is that the wing on an airplane is relatively rigid and supports the weight of the aircraft by its structural strength, but the helicopter's blades are much more flexible, relying on the centrifugal force imparted to them to support the weight of the aircraft. If the revs drop too low, the rotor blades will simply fold up like the spokes of an umbrella in a gale, and the helicopter will fall out of the sky. On the other end of the scale, if the revs are allowed to climb too high, the blades are likely to break loose from too much centrifugal force, with a similarly undesirable consequence.

For these reasons, holding the revs constant in a helicopter was just as vital as maintaining forward speed in an airplane, and that became the pilot's first reflex. Perhaps the most significant difference was that in a helicopter, particularly in the mountains, a pilot no longer tried to land into wind all the time. The direction of the wind was always a factor, but the prime concern was to land in a position from which he could take off again.

There were other problems peculiar to mountain flying in the helicopter Carl was using. As he climbed, the air became thinner, giving less lift to the rotor blades. At the same time, since the Franklin engine was a normally-aspirated engine—that is, without a supercharger—the density of the mixture going into the engine diminished with altitude, which in turn meant less and less power. In other words, given a short clearing, he could take off with two passengers at sea level, but he could not do so at, say, 4000 feet.

The technique Carl eventually developed was to land in a position from which he could literally throw himself off the mountain and, helped by gravity, pick up enough forward speed to fly to the next landing. In retrospect, the technique seems obvious. At the time it must have taken considerable courage to put it into practice. By the time Okanagan Air Services had been contacted by a provincial government department to experiment with the helicopter in the mountains, Carl was ready to demonstrate that it could be done, even though he still had a great deal to learn.

The genesis of this venture is intriguing because the suggestion actually came from a university student on a temporary summer job. E.R. McMinn, now Director of Surveys and Mapping in the provincial government, recalls the exact beginnings: "In 1947, on my first survey job up in Terrace, we had a university student on the crew, and we'd gone out to do a little practice mountain climbing to see how the crew could handle it. We got up on top of a hill and I said, 'My God, it's taken us five hours to get here, and look at it—you could land a bomber up here.' The kid looked around. He said, 'Well, why don't you use one of these new-fangled things, a helicopter?' We all laughed about that. But when we got back to camp, we mentioned it to the party chief, Gerry Emerson. He was a really bright and resourceful person, and instead of laughing he took to the idea and followed it up."

The Topographic Survey crews were engaged in triangulation. Using theodolites to measure angles and distances, they were laying out a survey grid from which the cartographers could make maps. In triangulation, the longer the base line the more accurate the grid and the less work has to be done to complete it. Obviously, the higher they could place their instruments, the longer the base lines. But getting high with all their equipment was backbreaking work on foot; so they were naturally interested in any machine which might ease the burden.

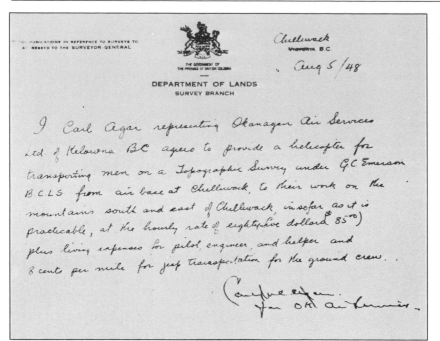

*One of the first British Columbia Government contracts for helicopters was with Okanagan in 1948. (Okanagan Helicopters Collection)*

*(Left) New instruments and techniques were introduced as helicopter use increased in topographic surveys. In the left foreground is a tellurometer, which transmits a signal to a dish mounted on the helicopter, in this case an Okanagan Hiller 12-E. By measuring the time it takes for the signal to return, distance can be determined. The theodolite on the right measures the angle. Towers such as the one in the right photo were used in triangulation. It was important to establish these benchmarks as high as possible. Helicopters on occasion replaced them by simply hovering at the required height over the spot. (British Columbia Ministry of Environment)*

Gerry Emerson, with the support of the Surveyor-General, Norman Stewart, contacted Okanagan Air Services and arranged a contract for 25 hours of flying time during the late summer of 1948. They were to work on a map sheet in the Chilliwack area—in the Wahleach Mountain Range which runs southeast towards Chilliwack Lake. The cost was to be $85 an hour for the helicopter. It is interesting to note that Carl Agar was earning only $350 a month for this dangerous experimental flying, and Alf Stringer only $300 for maintaining the machine.

"Carl Agar and Alf Stringer arrived with their machine at Chilliwack airport," Ernie McMinn recalls, "and we went down and looked at it. Gerry showed Carl on the map where he wanted to go. He wanted to land on a mountain called Cheam Peak. Carl went off by himself and had a look. When he got back, he said, 'Fine, I found a spot back there and landed on it. Had to chase a black bear off it first, but it's no problem.'"

In fact, Carl had spent some time working out the best procedure for a landing and takeoff from a small, frozen lake in a cirque at the 5300-foot level. First he approached it at 40 miles an hour, peeling off while he still had room to drop off the edge of the cirque and pick up speed again if he needed to. Then he tried it at 30 miles an hour. Finally, he decided to commit himself, gradually dropping his speed as he let down until he arrived at the ice surface just as he reached zero forward speed. He was anxious about the strength of the ice at that time of year, but on wheels, it provided a temptingly flat landing surface. As it turned out, the ice was sheltered from the sun most of the time and bore his weight. The takeoff was a little more difficult, but by slightly over-revving the engine he got away all right.

Norman Stewart, the Surveyor-General, was his first passenger. They landed on the ice again but decided it was not reliable for repeated landings. They climbed up onto the ridge in front of the lake, found a flat spot, and cleared away the rocks until they had a satisfactory landing site. Carl left Stewart there and went back for Gerry Emerson and then Ernie McMinn. As Ernie describes it: "We got out on the ridge and had to climb about half a mile to get to the mountain top. In fact, as we realized later, the ridge Carl had chosen was far from ideal for a helicopter landing. It was at the foot of a glacial cirque —a ridge of gravel in front of a little lake with a wall of ice behind it. And of course the cold air was coming down off the ice like a waterfall. Not a good place for any kind of flying machine. Anyway, we climbed the mountain and on the way up we walked into the remains of a Lodestar. It had piled into the mountain in '42, I think. It was an Air Force machine and the engines were burned right into the rock. Just a pile of aluminum down at the bottom of a cliff. We got back to the landing and Carl picked us up just as the fog was rolling in. The weather really socked in. I think we were grounded in the pouring rain for the next five days."

Thus began the first of many helicopter survey operations in which Ernie McMinn was involved. He remembers being excited rather than nervous on those first experimental flights: "We thought it was a great thrill, sailing over the ground at 60 miles an hour. We could see how long it would take to walk through it; if you could walk a mile an hour you were doing well. And Carl didn't like heights. The only place he felt safe was sitting in his flaming helicopter! Getting out on the ridge of a mountain, he'd walk over to the edge and suck his breath in. . . . But we had a lot to learn.

"The biggest problem to begin with was the wheels. The helicopter had four little wheels, and they were a menace. It was awfully hard to find somewhere really flat to land—and if you landed on a slope, the machine would start to roll. There were no brakes. I remember once they tried to take off from the top of a snow slide and couldn't quite make it so they had to land again on the slope and rolled all the way down the snow-bank, about three or four hundred yards. Eventually, they reached a flat space and stop-

*(Left) Ernie McMinn, shown here on the side rack of a 47-D1, was involved with helicopters almost from the beginning of their operations for the Topographic Surveys Branch. (Right) Gerry Emerson, shown here refuelling the B3, understood the potential of helicopters in topographic survey work and appreciated the limitations as well. (British Columbia Ministry of Environment)*

ped. After a good deal of soul searching, they took of again. But still, apart from the wheels, the biggest problem was getting off with a load when you were high—up about five or six thousand feet. You had to carry a theodolite and tripod, which weighed about 35 pounds, and a camera, which in those days weighed about 30 pounds. So Carl soon came up with the idea of landing on the edge of a drop-off. He'd take some extra revs. I can remember some of those takeoffs . . . the revs were dropping back from 3600 to about 2800, and the thing was falling, but it was falling clear, and gradually we'd pick up the revs again.'' [Clearly, Carl Agar did not pay much attention to the maker's red line on the tachometer: 3200 was supposed to be the maximum.]

Alf Stringer responded to the problem of the wheels by improvising his own braking system. He cut strips from an old car tire and wedged them between the axle and the tire. This worked after a fashion, but they had advised Bell of this problem: Bell responded by putting hydraulic brakes on the wheels. Stringer advised them at the same time that the real answer was some sort of fixed undercarriage; the helicopter didn't really need wheels, except when it was being moved in and out of a hangar. The first skid gear appeared in 1949, and after that only very large helicopters had a wheeled undercarriage.

The other advantage of the skid gear, when it appeared, was that it lent itself to fixing loading racks on either side of the helicopter. Trying to carry tripods, instruments and back-packs in the small cockpit was obviously unsatisfactory. Meantime, the first experimental operation with the Topographic Survey was a qualified success. The weather was bad much of the time, and they did not accomplish as much as they had hoped. Nevertheless, they managed to occupy eight or ten survey stations and needed no more persuading that the potential was there.

From Chilliwack, Carl and Alf went straight to another job at Knight Inlet, a short job, only 12 hours of flying; but it broke new ground again. It was an aerial timber cruising survey, and the customer was delighted with the results, the ease with which they could pick out routes for the cruisers to travel on the ground, and the simplicity of deciding where logging roads should be constructed.

That was the end of the second season, in most ways a very successful one. They had progressed from simple agricultural spraying to a more versatile role for the helicopter. This in turn meant that some firm decisions had to be made during the coming winter.

# Okanagan Air Services: From Orchards to Mountains

*No one knew at the time what the Kitimat project was*
*about—we had no idea; it was a hush-hush deal.*

BARNEY BENT

Alf Stringer was boarding with Carl Agar and his wife, Anne, in Penticton during the winter of 1948, and they spent endless hours discussing the future. They had already concluded that aerial spraying was out. Now they decided that the future lay in competing with the horse—the packhorse trains which had always been used in the summer to take people and supplies into remote areas for surveying, mining exploration or timber cruising. By now, too, they realized the problems of their isolation in the Okanagan Valley. To win the sort of contracts they were beginning to contemplate, they needed to be closer to the seats of industry and government: Vancouver for the one; Victoria for the other. They settled for the former, renting hangar space at Vancouver airport in the spring of 1949. The company was still in the red.

The year began with two jobs: some mining exploration at Herbert Arm, operating from Tofino on the west coast of Vancouver Island; and the building of the Palisade Lake Dam in the mountains north of Vancouver, which was to augment the city's water supply. The latter was particularly valuable because it was such a visible operation. People in greater Vancouver could see the helicopter at work; at least some of them must have begun to realize its potential in their own fields.

For this job Okanagan Air Services had hired an ex-Skyways pilot, Paul Ostrander, to fly the second helicopter, while Carl flew CF-FZN on the mining job. Between them they flew long hours, moved many people and a great deal of equipment, and did much to bring the helicopter from being a curiosity into the realm of genuine utility. But a fundamental economic problem still faced them: they were only working in the summer, perhaps from June until early September. How to survive the seven months of winter with helicopters sitting idle in the hangar?

Nevertheless, things were beginning to look up, and in a letter to David Forman, Manager of the Bell's Helicopter Division, dated July 7, 1949, president Douglas Dewar was able to say: "You will be interested in knowing that we have just concluded a contract on a twelve month basis with the B.C. Electric Company and the Greater Vancouver Water District; for the former we will make a monthly patrol of their power lines, and for the latter we expect to move 500,000 pounds of construction materials to their new dam site at the head of Capilano.

"We are also concluding a contract with the Provincial Government Mapping Division for a topographical survey in difficult country in Northern B.C., following a similar successful operation last year."

They were busy and enjoying the satisfactions of accomplishment if not yet much in the way of financial reward. When Carl finished his Tofino job, he at once did some more timber cruising with the company he had worked for the previous fall, this time round Elaho Lake, north of Squamish. From there he went to Lytton to fly two geologists,

McKenzie and Warren, to a landing close to the 8000-foot level of Mount Gott, where he left them with their camping and prospecting gear. While he was in Lytton, he received a message to return to Vancouver and meet what turned out to be one of the most important customers he was ever to meet—Wilfred Heslop, a professor of civil engineering at the University of British Columbia, who was acting as a consultant to B.C. International Engineers. Carl took him for demonstrations in the helicopter in and around the mountains on the north shore. Heslop had little to say at the time, but he asked Carl to meet him in Terrace on August 31 for two or three weeks of flying.

Meanwhile Paul Ostrander was more than pulling his weight on the Palisade Dam job, flying as many as 30 round trips a day, carrying everything from lumber to nails to concrete, together with a concrete mixer. The mixer bowl weighed 400 pounds and became the first sling-load to be carried beneath a helicopter in B.C. A landing platform was constructed with a hole large enough to allow the bowl to be lowered into it. The helicopter landed above it. Four wires were slung from each of the undercarriage legs and hooked onto the bowl, which was then eased out of its hole in the platform and flown up to the dam site.

While this was going on, Carl left for Hazelton to begin the operation with the Topographic Survey people mentioned in Dewar's letter to the Bell company. Although he did not know it at the time, this was the first phase of the Survey's plans for a three-year project, under the direction of Gerry Emerson, to cover the area from Hazelton up to Atlin. Seven weeks later, with one Topo job finished, he was requested to go to the Indian village of Kitimat to assist Ernie McMinn, in charge of the government mapping project of the valley. After three months of difficulties with bad weather, rain forest and river crossings, the project was completed in 11 hours flying time. Then Carl flew to Terrace for his pre-arranged meeting with Heslop. With him, he returned to Kitimat, where a stock of fuel and oil for the helicopter had been landed by boat during the summer. They worked from there for the next two weeks.

This was the beginning of the Aluminum Company of Canada's Kitimat project which, if not actually the largest, was certainly one of the largest industrial development projects undertaken in British Columbia. It was also the turning point for both Okanagan and the entire helicopter industry.

Luck was with them right from the start. Barney Bent remembers it with a gleam of satisfaction in his eye: "No one knew at the time what the Kitimat project was about—we had no idea; it was a hush-hush deal. However, Carl met Professor Heslop at Terrace on the appointed day, and they were extremely fortunate with the weather; they had about two weeks of absolutely CAVU [ceiling and visibility unlimited] weather—which is certainly not a common occurrence in that area. As it turned out, the engineer was looking for a route for the power line. They had pretty well established from aerial photographs where they were going to locate the dam and hydro generating station, but the big question mark was the routing of the power line from Kemano to Kitimat. Carl flew them over some 13 potential routes in the two weeks they were together.

"They flew every day for long hours and they not only covered the power line routes, but also the lake areas where they were planning to reverse the existing flow of the drainage with their dams. They did so much work that everybody concerned was completely satisfied with the operation of the helicopter. They estimated they had saved one year, and possibly a good two years of engineering in that two weeks of clear flying. As a consequence, they assured us that if this project did go ahead, we were right in there, solid —and from day one. And the Kitimat project was the big break for Okanagan because it got us over the problem of seasonal flying. From now on we could plan, hire our crews, train them and know we were going to get a steady income. It made all the difference."

*This 1949 photograph of a Topographic Surveys Branch crew was taken north of Hazelton in the Kispiox River Valley. Carl Agar is sitting on the rack directly below the rotor mast. To his left are the cook and Frank Speed. Gerry Emerson is standing behind Speed. The other men were locals hired for the job. (British Columbia Ministry of Environment)*

While this was going on, an interesting development had taken place in Vancouver. Okanagan Air Services had been approached by a well known mining entrepreneur who had asked for comprehensive details about helicopter operations. Confident that another job was in the offing, they gave him all the information he wanted. A week or two later, management discovered that this individual was setting up a rival helicopter company. The new company never materialized, but the incident created some excitement. The next development was that Ostrander returned to Ontario, and Carl had to find a replacement. He would have to train somebody. Bill McLeod, the man he chose, was a seasoned fixed-wing bush pilot whose background, since it was so typical of a post-war bush pilot, is worth recording in some detail.

McLeod was born in Nanoose, but his parents soon moved to Ladysmith where he was educated. The year after he graduated from high school, he took a course in aircraft engineering with a small company called the Brisbane Aviation School in Vancouver. It was a correspondence course lasting for nine months, after which he completed three months of practical training and promptly went to work for a flying school called Foggin Flying Services. While working as an engineer for the flying school in 1939, Bill learned to fly in a Fleet 2, the same machine which now hangs in the entrance to the Modern History Gallery in the British Columbia Provincial Museum.

By now, the war had started, and Bill volunteered for the RCAF. He could not get in as aircrew because at that time the RCAF required at least two years of university education for potential pilots. So he joined as an aero-engine mechanic, went to work in an Elementary Flying Training School and promptly applied to remuster to pilot.

After completing his aero engine mechanic's training at St. Thomas, Ontario, he was posted to Ucluelet on the west coast of Vancouver Island. Here he worked on Stranraer flying boats until his reclassification came through and he was posted in turn to an Initial Training School in Edmonton, an Elementary Flying Training School in High River, and a Service Flying Training School in Calgary. From there he learned to instruct in Arnprior before finally ending up as an elementary flying instructor in Fort William.

Bill was next sent to Abbotsford, in the Fraser Valley, where he met Carl Agar, Com-

*The configuration of the Okanagan Bell 47-B3s changed dramatically during their operational lives. The covering has been removed from the tail boom of CF-FZN, a "harp" has replaced the tail skid, and skids have replaced the wheeled landing gear. Later a full bubble was added. The aircraft then differed little in appearance from more recent model 47-D1s in service. (Bill McLeod)*

manding Officer of the flight to which he was posted. Teaching students in Tiger Moths and talking endlessly as pilots do about flying, they got to know each other rather well. Then the war ended, and each went his own way—Carl to found the Penticton Flying Club, and Bill to run a small flying club for BC Airlines in Vancouver.

Bill's next move was to Queen Charlotte Airlines as a pilot on Stranraers. Later he flew Norsemen and Wacos. In 1948, he moved up to Prince Rupert to open and manage a base there. This period of coastal flying broadened his experience tremendously: six days a week into the Queen Charlotte Islands; one day a week into Alice Arm and Stewart, interspersed with unscheduled charter work which might take him almost anywhere in the province. Flying the West Coast in an aircraft with only basic instruments was at once the purest and perhaps the most difficult flying in the world. Much of the year, if you didn't fly in the rain, you didn't fly at all. The coast is a baffling maze of inlets, sounds, bays, arms, islands and canals; and if the pilot could see more than half a mile ahead, he felt as a motorist does after emerging from the rush hour traffic of a city into a quiet country lane.

But clearly there were compensating factors, and when Bill left QCA it was because of personal problems and not because he disliked the job or the company. As he said: "I left QCA and came down to Vancouver with nothing in mind, really—I didn't know what I was going to do. In the first three days I was offered five different jobs. The aviation community was still relatively small and you got to be pretty well known. One of the people to offer me a job was Carl Agar—so this was where the helicopter thing started.

"We met in the coffee shop (where so much of the business of flying seems to have been transacted), and Carl said to me, 'How would you like to fly a helicopter?' I looked at him to make sure he was serious. He was. 'I've never even seen one,' I replied. And I hadn't—I had never even seen a helicopter at that stage of my career. And he said, 'Well, you come over with me and have a look. I've got a little job to do. You can come along with me on this job and that'll give you an idea of what you can do with a helicopter.'

The job turned out to be an effective demonstration of the versatility of a helicopter: "There was a big smokestack at one of the mills, over on the Fraser, and they had to hang a rope on it—a hook attached to an endless rope which would drop down and allow the steeplejacks to climb the stack and pull up the equipment they needed to work on it. So I climbed into this stupid machine—at that time I figured it was a stupid machine —it was the open cockpit Bell 47-B3 with the four wheels. They had had a hook manufactured, a home-made thing with a sort of a loop on the bottom and a long arm welded to it so I could reach out and clip it over the edge of the steel chimney. The rope went through the loop, and I had the rest of it, a big coil of heavy rope, in my lap.

"So we took off and chugged off along the Fraser. There was a nice brisk wind blowing from the west, about 25 miles an hour, which gave us a bit of added lift. Carl steamed up alongside this smokestack and I found I couldn't handle the pole sitting down. I had to put the rope on the floor, undo my seat belt, climb half out of the machine and put one foot on the wheel leg to hold the pole properly. Anyway, I got the hook on, picked up the rope and threw it down and got back into my seat. Then I realized that the long handle of the hook was against my stomach and if Carl started to move forward I was going to end up with a bad stomach-ache. So I got back out again, held on to the door frame, put my foot against the smokestack and gave a good shove. The machine moved away and the handle dropped out. I sat down again and gave Carl the thumbs up and away we went. By the time we got back to the airport, I was thinking: 'Anything you can do that with, I've got to learn to fly.''

Bill McLeod was trained by Carl Agar in the winter of 1949-50. When he left to work on his first operation he had some 60 hours of helicopter time. But his mountain flying experience consisted of four demonstrated landings and perhaps 20 landings and takeoffs on his own, all on three locations.

The job he started on was the Topographic Survey operation, beginning where the previous year's crew had left off. They started north of Kispiox, up the Nass River, at a place called Brown Bear Lake, and worked north up the Nass Valley to the Bell-Irving River. This was the first time the Topographic Survey had worked entirely with air support. Fixed-wing aircraft took in the equipment and supplies; helicopters moved the surveyors from one occupied survey station to the next. They had finally abandoned the pack horse.

Bill recalls the encouragement he received at the start of this, his first helicopter operation: "When the machine was loaded up and I was ready to leave for Kispiox, Carl came out and shook hands with me and he said: 'Well, Bill, remember one thing—if you get through this season without breaking a helicopter, you'll be the first man who's ever managed to do so.' With those happy words ringing in my ears, I climbed into the machine and took off. As it turned out, I did manage to get through that first season without breaking a helicopter, but I sure scared the hell out of myself a few times.

"You see, the truth was, you had to learn a whole new ball game. Remember that in an airplane you're trained right from day one to approach a landing, and to take off, into wind. If you persist in this in a helicopter in mountain terrain, you're dead—you're going to kill yourself; it's just that simple. Because it means that if you're approaching a mountain and you're into wind, you're also in a down draft. If you do that, pretty soon you'll find yourself looking up at the place you were going to land, instead of down at it. So you get a few more grey hairs and you scare yourself a couple of times and you say, there's got to be a better way, and you develop these ways. You approach downwind and turn into wind at the last minute—something like that.

"An awful lot of what I learned that first season wound up in the mountain training manual Okanagan produced, because I wrote a lot of it. But only after I'd discussed my experiences with Carl Agar. That was Carl's great talent: he had a very special ability to talk to a pilot after the pilot had had some shaky experience and reduce it to its elements. He seemed to be able to see through what you were saying to the essence of what had happened. I guess this came from his long experience as an instructor. I think it was this ability to sort out the meat of an experience and then analyze it that made Okanagan Helicopters what it became.

"You see, the learning experience had to depend on making mistakes—that was the only way you could learn. If you're going into the unknown and there's nobody to guide you, you're going to make mistakes and, if you survive, you hand your knowledge down to others so that they won't make the same mistakes. The trouble is you have to go through some awfully hairy experiences to start with.

"I'll give you one example. I had landed on a ledge at about 6500 feet. There was a short cliff on one side and a sheer drop on the other, and the ledge would be about, oh, perhaps 150 feet. I landed about 60 feet in from the edge on a nice flat spot. On this particular day, I landed facing the cliff. What I learned then was that you never land unless you have figured out how you are going to take off again. Remember, we were at 6500 feet, and the only way you can get back into the air at that height is to over-rev the engine and jump off the edge. You'll lose your revs, but after picking up airspeed for a thousand feet or so, you'll pick up your revs again as well. But this time I did my jump takeoff too far from the edge. The front of the machine was going to go over the edge all right, but I knew the tail wasn't. I was already losing revs by the time I realized this. I shoved hard forward on the stick and then kicked on full rudder. I cartwheeled over the edge—cartwheeled so far that I was inverted at one stage and then I pulled out and got clean away with it. Right there, it was another few grey hairs. But after that I always landed very close to the edge of a drop off. And I always jumped sideways off a ledge."

When he had completed the Topographic Survey contract for the season, McLeod's next job was to fly men and equipment into the Reco Copper Mine. Although this was a small job, it was important because the take off and landing site was at Laidlaw, some 15 miles west of Hope, right along the Trans-Canada Highway. Like the Palisade job, it was very visible and attracted a lot of attention.

By this time Jock Graham had joined the company. He was an ex-Royal Air Force mechanic who had been working, like so many of the early staff, for Queen Charlotte Airlines on the diverse fleet it had assembled (insiders said that QCA stood for Queer Collection of Aircraft). Graham was based in Vancouver and so, by now, was Okanagan Air Services. It had leased a corner of a hangar and applied for certification of it as a permanent base. Graham, who worked in the same hanger, became intrigued by the curious machines Stringer and Agar were working on. He was single, with nowhere particular to go in the evenings and took to visiting them when his own work was finished.

He remembers the first meeting because it seemed to exemplify their ability to handle problems without getting excited. Carl was running up a machine after a transmission overhaul. The engine had to be run for about an hour, after which filters were pulled and checked to see if there was any metal in them—metal shavings would indicate that something was amiss in the transmission. The covering over the tail boom had been removed and a large and determined swarm of bees had settled on the boom. The bees weren't troubling Carl in the cockpit, so they finished the run up, shut down and went to find a beekeeper to remove the swarm before attempting to check the filters.

Some months later, with the Kemano contract in their pockets, Alf Stringer and Carl Agar decided to offer Jock Graham a job. He accepted, and his apprenticeship was to rebuild the second helicopter, the wrecked CF-FZN which had been bought from the insurance company the previous winter and shipped by rail from Winnipeg. Apparently, they all spent a great deal of time in and around the hangar, often sleeping in a sleeping bag on a couch. It was a time of excitement and tension for them all. The future looked inviting, but none of them had enough experience to be sure that the helicopter would do all the things they were planning. Now they were setting up a formal company structure and had to start looking for other help besides pilots and engineers.

Ada Carlson recalls how she was hired: "My husband was a vocational teacher in Vancouver and somebody from Okanagan phoned him to ask if he could find them a stenographer. He said he couldn't and mentioned it to me when he got home. I said, 'Why didn't you suggest me?' He said, 'Well, you're too old.' Anyway, he phoned them back the next day and said I was a good steno and they told him to send me over. That's how I became their first secretary in Vancouver. It wasn't much of a job to begin with —just a corner of the old Queen Charlotte Airlines' hangar. They didn't even have a ladies' washroom; I had to go across to the airport terminal.''

Carl's widow, Anne, remembers more clearly than anything else the difficulty her husband was encountering in his attempts to raise working capital, particularly from the more affluent members of the community. Both she and Ada recall that Douglas Dewar, a millionaire recently retired as United States president of the accounting firm of Peat Marwick Mitchell, was also very much a Scotsman. As Ada put it: ''He did have some money in, but it was really a small amount. I was amazed when I got there to find out that one director had one share, and somebody else had a share, and it was nothing, you know.''

Ada Carlson stayed with the company as an executive secretary until her retirement in 1963. When Okanagan's prosperous years began, she remembers that Carl decided to have a large and attractive house built on the corner of Angus Drive and Seventy-First Avenue in Vancouver. Typically, he was determined that it should be well built, plumb and true, and he asked his engineers for an accurate carpenter's level so that he could check construction as it progressed. His staff provided one, but only after they had rigged the bubble to give a false reading. We have no record of Carl's relations with his builder after that. Meanwhile, Jock Graham stayed in Vancouver, making forays to the Reco Copper operation near Hope to do maintainance, and attending to the other helicopter working on the Palisade job. Then came Kemano.

The Aluminum Company of Canada's Kitimat project was an imaginative one, but it was not greeted by everyone as enthusiastically as it was by helicopter operators. Many people were concerned about its effects on the environment. Dams were to be built on Whitesail Lake, Des Lake, the east end of Tahtsa Lake, and at the Canyon dam site on the Nechako River, reversing the flow of several large lakes which normally drained into the Nechako River. This created a 335-square-mile reservoir, the water from which was released through a 10-mile tunnel through the mountains from the west end of Tahtsa Lake, which in turn dropped it 2600 feet into the powerhouse turbine generators at Kemano. The powerhouse itself was constructed in a giant cave excavated from the mountain. The power generated would then be transmitted to the aluminum smelting plant to be built at Kitimat.

For Okanagan Air Services, though, it was a time of expansion and optimism. The initial crew, pilot Bill McLeod and engineer Jock Graham, arrived in 1951, before the first barge-load of supplies had been brought in up the Gardner Canal. They began with a visit to a test tower which had been erected in Kildala pass the previous summer by Carl

*Ada Carlson (left) joined Okanagan when things were starting to look up. (Ada Carlson)*

*A substantial helicopter pad in the mountains; many were far smaller. (Alf Stringer)*

Agar. This was the pass through which Alcan was hoping to construct the transmission line. The tower was at 5000 feet, and it was to record the build up of ice over the winter. Evidently the tests were successful because that was the pass chosen for the transmission line.

Things moved quickly after that. Bill McLeod recalls the first few weeks: "When we went in on the Kemano project, my first commitment was for eight weeks. Our reason for being there was to move the survey crews. They were going in only two weeks ahead of the road construction crews, who were going to build 10 miles of road from tidewater on the Gardner Canal up to the actual powerhouse site on the Kemano River. The idea was that they could get the road surveyed up the valley and stay far enough ahead of the construction crews coming on their heels that they would have a surveyed line and a surveyed road to work on.

"I found that I was not only flying the surveyors, but I was flying all the construction people as well. At the end of eight weeks, you couldn't have got that thing (helicopter) out of there with a bulldozer. They'd have killed you if you had tried to take the helicopter away from them."

Jock Graham remembers it as a time of adjustment. He had not previously worked in the bush, so he was not sure what to expect. He and many others on the project needed to come to terms with the area and its people. For example, on their way to Kemano, they landed on a large scow in Butedale. Bill McLeod had gone to visit someone, leaving Jock to look over the machine before they continued on their next leg. An Indian strolled down to look at the helicopter. Jock addressed him in the Hollywood version of an Indian *lingua franca.* "How!" he said. "Heap big machine, eh?" The Indian studied the small Bell for a few seconds. "Mmm," he agreed gravely, "but not nearly as big as the Sikorsky S-51."

A United States Air Force B-36 bomber, en route from Alaska to Texas, had encountered severe icing. After it had lost two of its engines, 12 of the crew had baled out, landing on Princess Royal Island. Five more stayed on board. As was learned much later, they had jettisoned an atomic bomb during the emergency. The wreck of the bomber was found several years later near Prince George. The five remaining crew members were never found. The 12 on Princess Royal Island were rescued with the help of a Sikorsky S-51 helicopter. Presumably it landed at Butedale on its way to the search area.

The construction people experienced a similar culture shock. To begin with they worked off a scow tied to the shore of the Gardner Canal, living in a float camp rented from a logging company. McLeod's first task was to put out the survey crews so that they could survey the initial road line up to the Kemano site. George Smith, the surveyor in charge (who, in the course of time, became Jock Graham's father-in-law) went off to an Indian village to hire a crew to do the actual cutting. He sought out the Chief and, like Jock, spoke in a mythical argot. "You fit to cut trees for white man?" he inquired. "Yeah, okay", the Chief replied, "I presume you'll be paying union rates?"

While Bill was moving the line-cutting crews and the surveyors back and forth, Fred Snell came up with the other machine to join them. He went to work on the tunnel survey. Things went remarkably well from the very start. The performance of the helicopters lived up to their most optimistic expectations. In a matter of months, the pressure was on for more helicopters to meet the demands of the engineers and the surveyors.

Consequently, as the Kemano project swung into high gear, so did Okanagan Air Services. During the first six months of 1951, they earned their first profits, $10,000, and their first two machines were converted by Alf Stringer from wheels to skids. At the same time, he fitted the now familiar full Plexiglas bubble instead of the original windshield. They bought another helicopter, CF-FJA, from the Kenting company for $15,000 (this had been the first commercially licensed helicopter in Canada). Meanwhile, crew training proceeded apace. After D.K. "Deke" Orr and Fred Snell came Peter Cornwall, Leo Lannon and Don Poole as pilots; Sig Hubenig, Bill Smith and Gordon Askin joined Jock Graham as engineers. By the end of that year, they had three Bells, CF-FZX, CF-FZN and CF-FJA; and Alcan had bought two, CF-GZX and CF-GZJ, Okanagan having first offer if Alcan decided to sell them.

By now the concept of using the helicopter just to move the survey crews had been forgotten. Innovations began to emerge. For example, a large boatload of material had to be moved from the east end of Tahtsa Lake to the west end, where the tunnel would begin. The lake was still frozen, so the old spraying equipment was installed on one of the helicopters. A mixture of soot and coal oil was sprayed in a 50-foot swathe stretching some 18 miles along the ice. The black soot absorbed the heat from the sun; consequently the swathe thawed more rapidly and the boat was able to move some two weeks sooner. Another innovation was the installation of landing pads as construction fanned out for the various phases of the development. They had to be built on the sidehills of the mountains so that engineers and drill crews could keep up with a project which was already well ahead of schedule.

Such dramatic progress brought about by the helicopter was bound to attract attention in Canada and elsewhere. This resulted in some tension among the directors of Okanagan Air Services. Carl Agar, whose official position at this time was general manager, was eager to take advantage of the situation to expand. By now he was getting requests from Ottawa to train pilots to operate on icebreakers; the Army wanted mountain training for its pilots; geophysicists in the federal Department of Mines and Technical Surveys wanted a machine; the provincial Topographic Survey people wanted to expand operations; and numerous mining companies were making inquiries. The demand for more helicopters was so great that Agar was convinced that if Okanagan did not supply them, competitors would spring up to benefit from the pioneering that he and Alf Stringer had done. But Douglas Dewar was conservative. Capital costs required for expansion were formidable, and he wanted to proceed cautiously. There were some lively directors' meetings during this period, and in the end they reached a compromise. They did expand, but neither as fast as Carl would have liked, nor as slowly as Dewar would have preferred. History suggests that it was a successful compromise. They did not lose control through sudden over expansion, nor lose business to any competitor. In fact, their first competitor failed to appear until 1954.

In the meantime, much was happening to encourage everyone. Carl Agar was constantly in demand as a consultant or speaker; he was gaining almost month by month in public recognition which, although it was gratifying, made it difficult for him to keep pace with his workload. First, he was invited to attend an investiture in Victoria, where he was presented with the Air Force Cross, a decoration he had earned in 1945 but had not yet collected. Then in April 1950, when he was at Kemano, he learned that he had been awarded the McKee Trophy, the most prestigious award in Canadian aviation. This in turn resulted in an invitation to speak at the International Air Transport Association's annual convention at Harrison Hotsprings.

Carl had become a celebrity. Soon after he returned from Harrison Hotsprings, he was invited to be guest speaker at the annual convention of the Helicopter Association of America in Washington, D.C. Here he met for the first time Igor Sikorsky, father of the modern helicopter. They took to each other from the first, and Sikorsky arranged to have Agar sit beside him at the head table. This led to another development for Okanagan Air Services, the procurement of the first two Sikorsky S-55 helicopters. But we are jumping ahead of our story.

# CHAPTER 3

# Okanagan Helicopters: Kemano and New Horizons

*When the noise finally died down, I was still 30 feet from*
*the ground in the trees, inverted, swaying gently up and*
*down and listening to the pitter-patter of the rain drops.*
BILL McLEOD

But for some bulldozers parked in a clearing among the trees, the campsite at Kemano in the fall of 1951 looked much like the construction camps in photographs taken at the turn of the century. The campsite was situated on the flats formed by the confluence of two streams with the Kemano River. The rows of wooden-walled tents squatted like tiny, angular mushrooms beneath the mountains. But the inhabitants of this small canvas city, erected the previous year by the Morrison-Knudsen and the Northern Construction companies, seldom felt the weight of those brooding mountains pressing down on them. For the mountains were usually lost in the clouds which swirled in from the Pacific Ocean.

Normally the view was restricted to the muddy river and the dark, sombre trees, dripping with rain. All one could see of the mountains was an occasional sliver of snow in a deep gully, reaching up into the overcast. It was on just such a morning that Joan McLeod, wife of the Okanagan pilot, was tending the primus stove in her tent. She was baking an upside-down cake in the tin oven which surrounded the stove pipe. She remembers that oven with affection because in it she could cook large roasts of meat and serve everything from well done to extremely rare. This was important because, as she was the sole woman in the camp in the early days of the project, her tent was the only alternative to the company cook-tent. She found herself having to prepare a lot of meals.

Apart from the fact that Joan was an excellent cook, there was another reason why her meals were so popular. The newly created society of Kemano was very stratified: supervisors could only associate with other supervisors; workmen could only associate with each other. Yet in Joan's tent, because she was the wife of a helicopter pilot, the company could be mixed. It is an interesting fact, and one not easy to explain, that helicopter pilots and their families were nearly always acceptable in any gathering. For the moment, Joan found it satisfying because, as she points out: "There were some fascinating people up there, people recently over from Europe. There was one chap who was literally digging ditches. He was an Austrian. He had been a colonel—a very, very literate chap who got on awfully well with a lot of the others who were supervisors, and we could have him at the tent and the supervisors as well, and there was never any problem, whereas he couldn't invite them to his tent nor expect an invitation from them.''

Joan McLeod was born in Toronto, spent some years in England, then returned to be educated in her home town. Armed with a degree in modern languages, she grew bored with Toronto and headed west, with no plans for a vocation. She worked for a while in an advertising agency, one of whose clients was the largest flying company in British Columbia at that time, Queen Charlotte Airlines. The advertising agency went bankrupt and she moved to QCA as traffic agent, radio operator and dispatcher in Prince Rupert.

Here she met her husband, Bill, just before they both decided to leave QCA and head back to Vancouver.

The period before they were married, while Bill was taking his training as a helicopter pilot, was a lean one. Joan tried unsuccessfully to find a job, and they were forced to live on Bill's salary which, while he was training, was $200 a month.

But once Bill had made the transition from the QCA Stranraers, Norsemans and Rapides to helicopters, things began to improve. In Kemano in the fall of 1951 he had been working with the construction crew, putting in the road from tidewater to the new settlement. Now the project had expanded and he was flying construction crews into newly installed helicopter pads in the mountains. Work had begun on the tunnel from the west end of Tahtsa Lake and on the main excavation for the power house. The two helicopters, one flown by Bill, the other by Fred Snell, were constantly in demand.

Joan McLeod made a good start on her upside-down cake that day, but it was never baked. Just as she was about to put it in the oven, she heard a commotion outside her tent. She stuck her head out to see what was going on and saw the engineering supervisor sprinting towards her along the land between the row of tents.

''Where's Bill?'' he demanded as he reached her. ''Fred Snell's killed himself.''

''Fred's not flying today—Bill is.''

''Then where's Fred? Bill's killed himself.''

Not surprisingly, Joan abandoned her cake and followed the supervisor in his search for Fred Snell. Failing to find him, they returned to the river, where the accident had occurred. Standing on the far shore, looking depressed but obviously not dead, was Joan's husband. After shaking his head, he turned and disappeared into the trees again.

Bill recalls that it had been raining so hard that day that neither he nor Fred Snell had

*As always very humble, Okanagan crews at Kemano (left) felt obliged to record their achievements, including passengers scared, bulldozers lifted and lakes thawed. Here, clockwise from the top, are Bill Brookes, Deke Orr, Gordy Askin, Ivor Barnett, ''Frenchie'' (a Morrison-Knudsen employee) and John Porter. (Right) Joan McLeod, who to begin with had lived ''downtown'' in the middle of a row of tents, soon moved out to the suburbs of Kemano. Later, accommodation was in steel Quonset huts. (Gordy Askin, Bill McLeod)*

*Okanagan's 47-D1 CF-GGC on the Kemano project, 1953. (Alcan)*

flown: "That was a bad year. We had one of those flash floods up at Kemano. Horetzki Creek, which flowed down into the Kemano River, was rising at a rate of about a foot an hour and a log jam had developed. They were afraid the camp would be flooded. A bull-dozer went out to try to clear the jam and it dropped into a hole. There were three people on the 'cat.' One fell off and managed to swim ashore; the other two were up on the canopy, ankle-deep in the water. The water was still rising and two of the supervisors came to me and said, 'Those guys are going to drown; you'll have to get them off.' So I said okay, but here's where I made my mistake: I didn't go over and tell those guys on the 'cat' what to do myself—I told the others to tell them while I ran for the helicopter.''

The instructions Bill wanted relayed to the men on the bulldozer were to wait until he had put one skid on the canopy, then, and only after he had given them the nod, they were to climb into the helicopter, one at a time. Bill took the doors off and when he got to within two or three feet of balancing one skid on the canopy, one of the catskinners made a wild leap and grabbed the front of the skid. The helicopter dropped violently and the tips of the skids went into the water. The only thing Bill could do was to pull up hard on the collective (the control which makes a helicopter rise or drop vertically) and twist on as much throttle as he could. But the weight of the man on the right skid pulled the helicopter down and to the right. There was, as Bill says, "nothing on the right but trees" and he went barrelling right into them.

"When the noise finally died down," Bill recalls, "I was still 30 feet above the ground in the trees, inverted, swaying gently up and down and listening to the pitter-patter of the rain drops. The fellow who was riding the skid was still there; he was half in the machine and half out; he was sort of pinned. Of course the bubble was gone and I noticed the battery was smoking. You know those braided battery straps? Well, believe it or not, you can tear one of those apart with your hands if you're desperate enough.''

The over-eager passenger was unconscious. Bill's first attempt to get him out of the machine failed. So he climbed down to the ground and found a branch to use as a pry. This time he was able to free the passenger and get him down to the ground. It was a ticklish business because Bill was afraid the helicopter might break lose and come crashing down. He managed to work the passenger free, ease him onto his shoulder, and climb down to safety. The passenger recovered a few minutes later, but they were on the wrong side of the river and Bill emerged from the trees to see what was going on. What he saw made him shake his head in dismay after a minute or two, and turn back into the trees.

There were some 400 people on the far bank and they were in the grip of a remarkable panic. One man was rushing into the water with a first-aid kit. He would rush until the water reached his thighs, realize that he couldn't go any further, retreat to shore, only to rush back into the water again, sobbing with frustration. A little further along, somebody had backed a bulldozer with a logging boom on it up to the water. A man was standing on the logging boom with a coil of rope, hurling it towards the far bank. It never reached more than half way across the river, but doggedly he retrieved it, coiled it and tried again. An hour later he was still doing the same thing. ''It was just unbelievable,'' Bill recalls. ''All that crowd of people—it was mass hysteria.''

Joan McLeod, surrounded by panic, finally did the one thing that is effective for hysteria. She ran up to the engineering supervisor and booted him as hard as she could in the backside.

Shocked, he turned to look at her. ''What did you do that for?'' he demanded.

''To make you start thinking.''

It worked. The engineer sent for a mobile crane. They strapped a log to the boom, lowered it across the river and succeeded in rigging up a sort of bosun's chair which got Bill and his passenger back across the river, as well as the man still stranded on the bulldozer. Kemano at that time boasted a hospital of sorts and they were taken there to be treated. It turned out that Bill was more seriously damaged than his passenger. He had broken off the instrument pedestal in the helicopter with his shin, and he was in considerable pain and some shock. Joan McLeod, by her own account, still had a rough night ahead of her.

''The regular staff doctor was out on holiday and he had been replaced by a pathologist who had decided to take a busman's holiday in Kemano. He hadn't done any general practice work for some years. But he patched Bill up and gave him some pain killer which contained codeine. Later on we discovered that Bill was allergic to codeine. But at the time he seemed to settle down and we went back home to the tent. By now it was getting late, so I got Bill into bed and then joined him and went to sleep.

''Sometime in the small hours I woke up to find Bill standing with one foot on my face. He was talking very strangely, not very rationally, so realizing that something was obviously very wrong, I got up, wrestled him down onto the bed and got the dog to lie on top of him to keep him still while I went for help. I ran to the engineer's tent and woke him and he went for the doctor while I went back and lay on top of Bill with the dog to keep him still until the doctor arrived. This time the doctor gave him some morphine and Bill did finally settle down for the night.''

Fortunately Bill's injuries were not serious and he was soon flying again. But there were two more accidents that summer. In the first, a construction worker walked into the tail rotor of CF-GZJ and was seriously injured. Then, Fred Snell had an engine failure. He had to autorotate (the equivalent of a glide in a fixed-wing aircraft) into some rocks and, though he was unharmed, the machine was badly damaged. These accidents were accepted as more or less inevitable; they did not cause too much anxiety, except perhaps to the pilots involved.

But less than a year later there was an accident which caused a great deal of concern for everyone. Bill was fortunate to survive it: "I was just heading back out of the pass [Kildala] when the machine started to develop a very heavy bounce; it was bouncing up and down about a foot, and it kept getting worse. I was about 1500 feet above the ground when it started and I let down as fast as I could. Then the bubble broke; finally, the engine quit and the tail rotor let go—it was bouncing so badly the tail rotor drive-shaft tore right out of the transmission—and I had to dump collective. Even then, I was spinning. All the controls went; the whole bottom end of the engine fell out. I had cartons tied on the racks and they all flew off.

"I was lucky though; I hit on the only patch of snow in the whole area. It was about 80 feet wide and 100 feet long, on a steep slope. I hit right in the middle of it. I slid down and hung up on boulders. Eighty feet further on, there was a drop-off of some 500 feet down onto a glacier. When I stopped, I looked up and I could see the sun shining. I said, 'Boy, that's a nice looking landing field.' Because I really didn't expect to come out of that one."

Bill came out of the wreck with a cracked vertebra; his passenger suffered cuts and bruises but no broken bones. People on the spot were dismayed because, apart from the engine failure, there had been no mechanical problems worth mentioning. Jock Graham, who by this time was Okanagan's base manager at Kemano, was determined to find the cause. If he did not, pilots and their passengers would be nervous every time they took off. Jock describes his investigation:

"It was a broken yoke [the hub on top of the rotor mast to which the main rotor blades are attached.] Bell had come out with aluminum yokes to save weight, and they sent out a directive that, if you ever had a blade strike, you had to throw away the aluminum yoke. We had bought the machine, 'JAA, from another company and I went back through the log book. Sure enough, I found an instance where they changed the blades. The obvious question was, 'Why had they changed them?' It took me some time, but I managed to get in touch with the engineer working on the machine when they had changed the blades, and he admitted they had done so because the tip had hit an oil drum. They were a small outfit. They didn't want to spend the money on a new yoke, so they didn't throw it away."

Apart from accidents, the helicopter crews began to become restive about their salaries. Their dissatisfaction was brought into focus by a recent immigrant who spoke very little English and whose job was to clean up around camp and to wield a shovel when called upon. The labourer had heard that the pilots were earning $350 a month, while he was earning over $500. Everytime he saw the helicopter crews he would shake his head and begin to laugh. And now that some of the initial glamour was beginning to wear off and the danger becoming more apparent, the helicopter crews grew increasingly resentful. They had played a vital part in the accelerated progress of the whole project and at the same time were its lowest paid employees! This apparently led to some lively exchanges between Carl Agar and his fellow directors in Vancouver, particularly since profits, which had stood at $10,000 in June, had risen to $58,000 by the end of August 1951.

During this period, Carl Agar's connection with Igor Sikorsky began to pay off. For some time Alcan had been considering larger helicopters to move heavier equipment. Carl phoned Sikorsky and asked him if there was any hope of getting two S-55s, capable of loads up to 1500 pounds as compared to the 400-pound capacity of the Bells. There were two immediate problems: the Korean War was absorbing all the helicopters Sikorsky could produce; and the S-55 had not yet been certified for commercial operations. However, Sikorsky was confident that certification would be granted and, in late 1951, Jock Graham was sent down to the Sikorsky plant in Bridgeport, Connecticut, to take a

*Jock Graham, before long, was in charge of the engineering crew at Kemano. (Jock Graham)*

*The construction camp at Kemano, circa 1950. (Provincial Archives of British Columbia 1513)*

*CF-GHV was the first S-55 acquired by Alcan and operated by Okanagan. Here Carl Agar is shown chatting with pilot Bill McLeod. This S-55 was one of the earliest released by the US Government for commercial service. Almost the entire production run had thus far gone to the US military for use in Korea. (Alcan)*

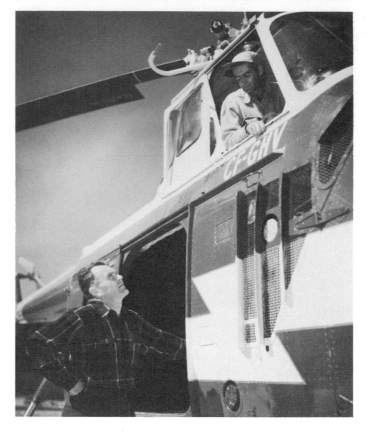

course on the S-55. When his course was almost completed, Carl Agar joined him for his conversion training.

The first certified commercial machine off the line was for Los Angeles Airways; the second would be Okanagan's. The first was ferried to Los Angeles in March 1952. The pilot gave a demonstration to the board of directors of the airline when he arrived. Unfortunately he experienced a tail rotor failure during the demonstration and several people were hurt. All S-55's were grounded until the manufacturer had solved the problem and incorporated a modification.

This delayed the Okanagan crew for three weeks, but finally, on April 10, they set off for Vancouver. Coincidentally, Bill McLeod had been visiting his wife's parents in Toronto, so he was picked up in Cleveland and, with instruction from Carl, did his conversion training by flying the machine back to Vancouver.

Okanagan's first S-55, CF-GHV, was taken straight to Kemano by Bill. With it he began to lift the materials for a camp of 60 men in Kildala Pass. Once the camp was established, he began to fly in the machinery and aluminum tower structures to complete the power line between Kemano and Kitimat. Moving lumber for the camp required another innovation, Bill recalls: "We rigged a rather novel idea for packing the lumber. At first we were packing it in bundles and slinging it. But that didn't work very well; it was slow and tedious. So what we did was rig a cable between the front wheels. Then we put the choker on the bundle of lumber so that it was very tail heavy on the sling. This meant that the front end of the load would snug up against the wire between the wheels, and the rear end would hang down below the horizontal. Then we had the sling cable rigged with a pressure switch so that a light came on in the cockpit as soon as

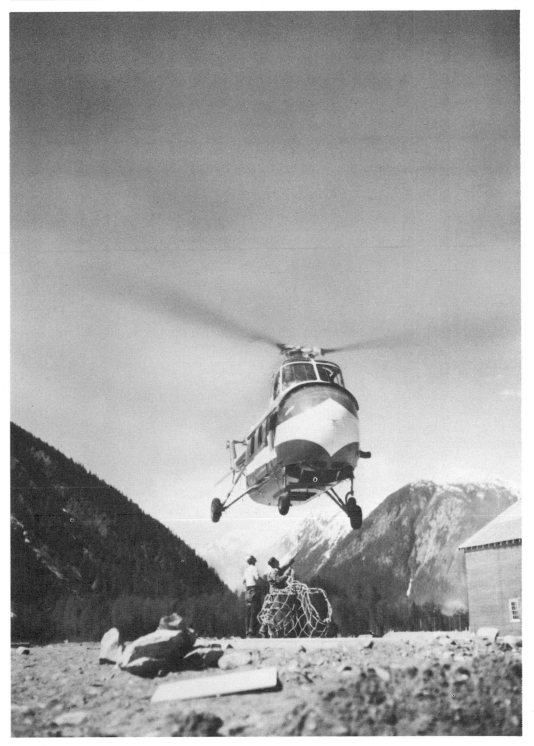

*The Alcan S-55s proved valuable at Kemano, their sling load being more than three times as great as the Bell 47-D1's. While owned by Alcan, these machines were identified by a silver ingot on the nose. Okanagan before long purchased the Alcan machines and subsequently operated more than 20-S-55s on the Mid-Canada Line. (Alcan)*

the load touched the ground and took some of the weight off it. We never had to stop. We kept moving at 5 to 10 miles an hour and kicked off the load as soon as the light came on. That really speeded things up.''

A few months later Alcan bought a second S-55 for Okanagan to operate and Deke Orr became its pilot. As with the Bells, the S-55s proved reliable. Jock recalls that they had one main transmission failure in the early days, but it did not cause an accident. Once the transmission had been replaced they had no more than routine maintenance to worry about.

By the end of 1952, the helicopter operation had settled down and become probably the biggest in North America. Alcan had constructed a hangar for the fleet which now amounted to two S-55s and four 47-Ds, with a crew of six pilots and six engineers.

Meanwhile for Joan McLeod, life, as it does, had become a little more complicated; in January 1952 the birth of her first child became imminent: ''In January our older daughter became very due, so it was decided that we'd better get out to the hospital in Prince Rupert. It was terribly rough; the ship could not come in and they couldn't get a tender out to her; instead, they brought the ship as close to the dock as they could and then swung out a net on a derrick and hoisted us aboard. It was even worse after Paddy was born and we came back. It wasn't quite so rough this time and they managed to get a tender out to us. We were taken down into the cargo hold, where they opened up the big cargo doors and laid a plank across to the tender. We had Paddy in a clothes basket and two men to push us off and two more waiting on the tender to grab us. Bill carried the clothes basket and made a mad dash and got across all right. I was still bent double at that stage of the game, but they threw me from one side and caught me on the other very handily. You travelled in style in those days.''

On her return to Kemano, Joan moved out of the wooden-walled tent into a Quonset hut, which was far less comfortable because condensation inside dripped steadily onto them in cold weather. When Paddy was nine months old, Bill was transferred to the Tahtsa Lake camp and Joan returned to Vancouver.

Bill joined her at the beginning of December for a Christmas break. Two weeks later Carl Agar phoned and apologetically suggested that it was urgent for Bill to return immediately to the Tahtsa Lake camp. As an inducement, he was to take Joan and the baby with him. Joan describes their arrival: ''We were in Tahtsa for Christmas, in a Quonset hut again. But it was colder at Tahtsa than Kemano, and foolishly they had bulldozed all the snow away from the walls so that we could walk around. This removed the insulation, and we were horribly cold inside. The baby was starting to crawl and stagger by that time. I used to take her out of bed in the morning and virtually sit her on the stove to dress her. I had cut down a pair of Bill's old grey socks and I'd pull those up to her hips; then the usual diapers and vest, followed by layers of sweaters, a snow suit, boots and mittens. Then I could put her down on the floor to crawl. But by this time the poor child was practically helpless—so many clothes she could hardly move.''

The McLeods' second child, Jean, was also born in Prince Rupert, in October 1953. With two children to look after, Joan left the Kemano project for good and returned to Vancouver. The helicopter crews were growing bored with the operation and started to look around for new worlds to conquer. Jock Graham wanted to be a pilot. He had a private pilot's licence and had unofficially flown the 55s a good deal in Kemano (they were equipped with dual controls and the pilots helped him as much as they could). But he needed a formal course and in spite of repeated requests, Carl always argued that he was more valuable to the company as an engineer. In the end, because he felt that he was being held back and that he might be able to get the training he wanted by joining another company, Jock accepted a job as technical representative with Pratt and

Whitney, manufacturers of the S-55 engine.

By 1954, work was beginning to wind down in Kemano. Alcan cut its fleet to one S-55 and two 47-Ds. The remaining machines, a 55 and two 47-Ds, were bought by Okanagan under their option. Fortunately Jock, in his new capacity, had contacts in Calgary by this time. He heard rumours that Shell Oil, carrying out exploration work on the Mackenzie River, was looking for something bigger than a Bell. He contacted Peter Leigh-Jones, executive assistant to Shell's president. At a breakfast meeting with Jones and John Stuart, Shell's chief pilot, Jock advised them to phone Glen McPherson, Okanagan's new president. Terms were quickly arranged and Okanagan had a three-month contract for their S-55.

Bill McLeod flew on this operation and describes it as the most enjoyable one of his career: "That was the first year that Shell had used a helicopter. They got a 55 and a Bell and I flew the 55. We did a preliminary geological survey of the Mackenzie mountains, starting at Fort Laird and working our way not quite to the Arctic coast. We were back in the Richardson range by the time we finished up. They were surveying a swathe of country approximately 40 to 60 miles west of the river, depending on where the pre-Cambrian rock occurred; in other words, it was soft rock geology. That was extremely interesting because we stayed only ten days to two weeks in any one location; then we moved on.

"They had three geologists, three helpers, my engineer (George Chamberlain), myself and a cook on our part of the operation. In the morning I would load all six of the geology crew and put two crews out to measure sections and take samples. Then I would travel with the third crew until it was time to pick up the others in the evening. Dr. Matthews from UBC was the geologist and I became a one-man classroom for him for the season. By the end of it, he would pick up a fossil, hand it to me and say, 'Well, what is it, Bill?'

*According to Alf Stringer, the original tail boom on this S-55 was damaged and, because the aircraft was needed quickly, Pratt and Whitney, Sikorsky representatives in Canada, sent a replacement out that was originally intended for the RCAF. It was later repainted. (Eric Cowden)*

and I'd reply, ''Oh, that's Middle Devonian; it's a Brachiopod.' I could reel it all off and it made the job much more interesting.

''That was one of those good years. Even the cook was good, and we were on the move all the time. We got to the point where the engineer and I slept in the helicopter. We didn't bother setting up the tent; we just rolled out our sleeping bags on the floor of the helicopter and went to bed at night—what there was of it.

''I had one engine failure and they had to come looking for me. No radio—the radio didn't work; usual thing in those days. I'd gone out and I had a magneto pack up on me. I tried to fly back to camp, but the engine got rougher and rougher; then she started missing on one cylinder, so I thought I'd better put her down because I still had some 60 miles of muskeg to go over. We were working out of Fort Norman at the time. It was rather odd; I put down on a river called the Redstone, on a sandbar which was composed of red and cream sandstone. The helicopter was painted cream and red. I had the best camouflaged helicopter you ever saw. And when I landed, there was thunderstorm activity and there were fires burning—little plumes of smoke all over the country.

''I did the usual thing: I laid out a square on the sand bar with a 'W' in it, meaning 'I need an engineer.' Then I gathered a big pile of brush to make smoke to compete with all the other smokes. Airplanes flew right over and never saw me. The fellow who finally found me was flying over a ridge 10 miles away, and he saw the sun glint on the plexiglas. Even then, he had trouble seeing exactly where I was. It wasn't a big deal. I was only out one night. The engineer came in and changed the mag—the drive had sheared —and we flew back to camp.''

Notwithstanding Bill's laconic description, it was a tough life. To prove that the helicopter really was practical, crews took considerable risks, worked very hard and, when they returned from the bush, played hard. The products of the grapevine and the barley field were not unfamiliar to them.

As a reaction to the disciplines of life in the bush, most of the early Okanagan crews were given to practical jokes; and Carl Agar, perhaps because he was so popular with his employees, was a favourite target. They delighted in jacking up the rear wheels of his car until they were just off the ground—then, when Carl jumped into the car to go home at the end of the day and spun his wheels futilely, he would look around to see a row of grinning faces at the windows along the side of the hangar.

Once, when the amber had flowed to celebrate Carl's McKee Trophy, someone sneaked out to the parking lot and chained the bumper of his car to one of the downspouts on the hangar wall. Fortunately the downspout tore loose before the bumper! On another occasion he nearly lost a valuable contract. He had gone up to do a quick test flight before driving downtown to meet a potential customer—a mining promoter who was considering using helicopters for a large exploration operation. While Carl was out flying, his crews were busy stuffing a deflated rubber helicopter float into his car. Then they inflated it. The problem for Carl was a difficult one: there was no way he could get into his car; he was in a hurry; but helicopter floats are very expensive and he didn't want to puncture the float with a knife. Thus he spent the next 15 minutes, surrounded by fascinated onlookers, desperately trying to worm his way far enough into the car to reach the valve and deflate the float.

As Carl became a celebrity (by the early fifties the media had taken to calling him ''Mr. Helicopter''), his crews made sure that he retained his sense of proportion. He hap-

*(Opposite) Bell 47-D1s, similar to those used on television's MASH series, were vital in the early days of the Kemano project. (Alcan)*

pened to be a short man and was constantly reminded of the fact. One day he had a new lawnmower delivered to the hangar, intending to assemble it there, where all the tools were available, before taking it home in the trunk of his car. The mower arrived in his absence and one of the engineers decided to open up the carton and have a look at it. As he did, an idea occurred to him. He cut some 18 inches off the mower handle, carefully buffed the edges to conceal the hacksaw marks and repacked the mower.

When Carl returned and assembled the mower, everyone in the hangar at the time (and there seemed to be more than usual for some reason) was bending over his work with unusual dedication. They intervened only when Carl went storming back to his office to phone the supplier. He was told that his loyal staff were merely trying to accommodate the mower to his size.

Apart from the practical jokes, though, both Alf Stringer and Carl Agar were individuals who tended to stand out in a crowd. Alf had a semi-military repartee which survived all the crises and occasional tragedies of a bush flying operation. When somebody's wife phoned and Alf answered the call, he would inform the husband that the "control tower" was on the blower. Peter Corley-Smith worked for him for nearly 15 years and was always puzzled by Alf's insistence on calling everyone "Colonel." When asked why, Alf would pass it off by changing the subject. It was only when we came to interview his wife, Lynn Stringer, that we discovered the reason for this idiosyncrasy. Alf had an indifferent memory for names. By calling everyone "Colonel" he avoided the difficulty so many of us face.

Another of the penalties Carl had to accept when he became a celebrity was that he had to attend conventions and conferences at which speeches, sometimes almost interminable speeches, were delivered. At a convention of the Helicopter Association of America in Los Angeles, one speaker grew fonder of his own voice as time went on, waxing philosophical about the advent of helicopters. He rehearsed the technical achievements up to date and the potential the future offered. He went on and on and on. Carl, who was seated at the head table, two seats away, had a bowl of daffodils in front of him. He picked one up and began to eat it slowly. When he had finished the last mouthful, he picked up a second and started on that. By now, everyone in the room was watching him. He had consumed three daffodils before the speaker, jolted from his euphoria, realized that he had more than lost the attention of his audience. When he turned to see what was happening, he closed his speech with a few brisk words and sat down. At all future conventions of the Helicopter Association of America, someone always made sure that Carl Agar had a bowl of daffodils in front of him when he took his place.

*Carl Brady (centre) was elected president of the Helicopter Association of America, succeeding Carl Agar in 1957. The photo, taken at the Sheraton-McAlpine Hotel in New York, also includes Elynor Rudnick of Kern-Copters, Bakersfield, California, a former president of the Association. (Carl Brady)*

Bell 47 B3-AG, CF-FZX, as it appeared on topographic survey work in 1949. The fabric covering on the tail boom created longitudinal stability problems in windy conditions. Covering the boom had nothing to do with aerodynamics; it was simply an attempt to make the helicopter more airplane-like.

Bell 47 G-3B-1, CF-VIH, in Vancouver Island Helicopters' "champagne and beige" livery of the early 1960s. There were subtle differences between the various submodels of the 47: the size and shape of the fuel tanks, the height of the instrument panels, the presence of a turbocharger, or the size and shape of the bubble could be used to identify the individual types by the well-informed.

Hiller 12E, CF-MHI, of Pacific Helicopters, c. 1964. This Hiller model was the main competition to the Bell 47 in the 1950s and 1960s and shared some of the same basic characteristics: the bubble-type cockpit enclosure, the two-bladed main rotor/single tail rotor configuration, and the flexibility to use either skids or floats. Okanagan also used this model but in a dark blue and orange livery.

\*Illustrations not to scale

*Sikorsky S-55, CF-FBW, purchased by Alcan and operated by Okanagan for the Kemano project, 1951. The engine, a radial type, was mounted in the nose behind "clam-shell" doors for easy servicing. The small aluminum ingot on the nose indicates Alcan's ownership of the aircraft. It was subsequently purchased by Okanagan.*

*Vertol HUP-3, 51-16622, of VU-33 Squadron, Royal Canadian Navy, Patricia Bay, 1962. This machine is shown in the two-tone grey livery typical of RCN aircraft of the period. The Navy White Ensign on the tail had only recently replaced the red, white and blue fin flash.*

*Vertol H-21A, 9611, of 121 Composite Flight, c. 1960. Initially 9611 appeared in natural metal finish but received this livery in the late 1950s.*

Bell 206B Jet Ranger, CF-MPI, the first helicopter operated by the Royal Canadian Mounted Police in British Columbia, 1974. While fixed-wing aircraft, largely bush types such as Beavers and Otters, are still used by the Mounties, helicopters, with their great operational flexibility, added an important dimension.

Bell 204B, CF-GAHN, of Alpine Helicopters, c. 1980.

Bell CH-135, 135107, of 408 Squadron, 1984. These machines, as well as Hueys, and Voyageurs, have frequently been used in training exercises involving ground forces in British Columbia.

*Aerospatiale SA 316C Alouette, C-FCAW, as it appeared between 1967 and 1984. Unlike their American counterparts, these aircraft are not equipped for rescue work, lacking hoist apparatus. The colours are now reversed, red predominating.*

*Sikorsky HH-52A, 1415, serving with the United States Coast Guard at Port Angeles, Washington, in 1984. These machines, which have performed well despite their power limitations, will soon be replaced by French-designed and built Aerospatiale Dauphin helicopters to be called Dolphins by the USCG.*

*Boeing Vertol CH-113 Labrador, 11303, of 442 Transport and Rescue Squadron as it appeared at the time of the* Prinsendam *incident, October 1980. With the completion of the SARCUP program, weather radar was added, altering the appearance of the nose. In this illustration, the "night sun" searchlight, normally fitted to the bracket below the nose, is missing.*

# Vancouver Island Helicopters Limited: Competition

*We went through eight pilots on that job. Some of them*
*would take one look at it and catch the next PGE train out.*
BOB TAYLOR

The first hints of competition to Okanagan Helicopters appeared in 1954. An aerial survey company in Ottawa, Spartan Air Services Limited, had started to use helicopters to provide the ground control—the surveyed heights and bench marks—it needed for mapping projects. Spartan, like Okanagan, expanded rapidly. By 1955 it had a fleet of more than 20 Bell 47s; in another two years it had a base in Calgary and was operating across the country.

Closer to home, on Vancouver Island, a young man called Ted Henson was watching the success story across the Strait of Georgia with increasing interest. Ted had been in the RCAF, hoping to become a pilot, but joined too late in World War II to achieve this ambition. Returning to Victoria after his discharge, he began work as an automobile mechanic. Then he suffered a bout of pleurisy, and while being treated in the Royal Jubilee Hospital met and fell in love with Lynn, a trainee nurse. Lynn abandoned her nursing career to marry Ted and went to work as a dental assistant, while Ted, with the help of a friend, Ron Page, managed to finance the purchase of a small Ercoupe monoplane in which he learned to fly and eventually earned his commercial pilot's licence. As it turned out, Ted did very little commercial flying in fixed-wing aircraft.

Times were hard for Ted, just as they had been for Carl Agar and Alf Stringer when they were trying to get back into aviation after the war. When he conceived the idea of getting into the helicopter business the problems of financing seemed insurmountable.

He began by writing the Bell Helicopter people to tell them about his ambitions. Bell responded by putting him in touch with their western representative in Los Angeles, Art Fornoff. Fornoff came up to Victoria to see Ted. Apparently satisfied that Ted was both sincere and capable, he arranged for an interview in Seattle between Ted and Bill Boeing Jr., son of the founder of one of the largest aircraft manufacturers in the world, who was forming his own helicopter company, Aero-Copters Incorporated.

Fortunately Ted and Bill Boeing hit it off and the immediate outcome was the formation of a partnership. At the time—this was in 1953—an American could hold only a 40 per cent interest in a Canadian company. Boeing's share of the company was to pay for Ted's helicopter pilot training and finance the purchase of the first machine, a Bell 47-G, with a down payment of $18,000. It was registered CF-IDX. Ted named the company Vancouver Island Helicopters Limited.

All this had been accomplished with relative ease. Now began the hard part—acquiring a licence to operate from the Department of Transport and the first revenue contracts. Lynn Henson (later Lynn Stringer) describes the problems: "It was the biggest battle of our whole life; it was so hard. You have to appreciate that we had no money. In September [1954] Ted had to quit his job as a mechanic because he had all this work with the business. The Liberals were in then and it was very difficult to get a licence. You had to prove that the traffic was there and that there was a public need for a helicopter service—which we did because we had done our homework. Then, when he put his application in, Ted made the mistake of asking for a protected base. This meant that no other operator could come within a 25-mile radius—and Okanagan fought that; they fought it very, very hard. Things were really tough for us. Ted had quit his job and my pay was very small. There we were in a little tiny house, 700 square feet, but with a big garden that kept us going."

Okanagan's objection to the founding of VIH had come as an unpleasant surprise, and while they waited with growing anxiety to see what the outcome of the objection at the Air Transport Board hearing would be, Ted was busy trying to raise capital to run the company. He went practically from door to door, urging people to invest—usually with indifferent success. The first principals, apart from Ted and Bill Boeing, were Ron Grant, a lawyer, and Dave Turnbull, a businessman whom Ted had met at the Victoria Flying Club.

At the same time, Ted was busy trying to find prospective customers. The B.C. Forest Service and B.C. Power Commission were his main targets. They appeared interested but they would not commit themselves. He received some encouragement from the newspapers, which followed his story with considerable coverage.

Okanagan's objections were carefully phrased. There simply wasn't enough business to justify another helicopter company; it was bound to fail. "We are not," they assured the Board of Transport Commissioners, "apprehensive of competition. Actually we welcome competition if it is shown to be in the public interest."

To which Ron Grant, Vancouver Island Helicopter's lawyer, responded dryly: "It is unusual for a business concern to set itself up as an economic watchdog."

The newspapers also referred to a mysterious American partner in the business (Bill Boeing, presumably), hinting at a threat to economic nationalism. At the same time they ran photographs of Ted and the brand new machine, CF-IDX, reporting that he was operating out of a field on Shelbourne Street. In fact, as Lynn points out, such operating as Ted was doing at the time was from the Howroyd strip in central Saanich. Joe Howroyd, always active in Victoria flying circles, was a friend and the landing strip was a very convenient base, at least for the moment.

In April of 1955, the long awaited letter arrived from the Department of Transport informing them that their application for an operating licence had been successful. Now Ted had to move from the casual phase of parking the helicopter on a friend's landing strip into some sort of hangar where proper maintenance could be performed. Lynn describes this move: "Ted was looking for a suitable place, with some room for an office, and he went out to the airport and here was this war-surplus hangar, packed high with old windows. They were using it as a warehouse. Every window on the hangar itself was broken. Just to look at it was so disheartening; but what else was there. So he said he'd take it. I think he paid $132 a month. He had to replace all the broken windows; then he cut a hole in the front of the hangar for a door so the helicopter could get in. There was just room for one helicopter and a little office."

Nevertheless, they were in business and Ted left in May, with his mere 25 hours of helicopter flying experience, to work for the B.C. Power Commission on the Homathko River, one of the roughest sections of terrain on the West Coast. Although the Power Commission was examining the potential for a dam and a generating plant on the Homathko, the actual work with the helicopter that first year was done for them by the Surveys and Mapping Branch of the provincial government. The engineering and environmental problems apparently could not be solved and no dam or generating plant was ever constructed, but the exploratory work continued for three years.

Ted was accompanied on this operation by Ted Protheroe, a fixed-wing engineer who had just earned his helicopter endorsement after a six-week course with Bell. Then, only a month or so later, Ted Henson suffered an accident, just as Carl Agar had on his first revenue operation, an accident which seriously damaged the machine.

Ted's accident was even more discouraging than Carl's encounter with the power transmission lines. He had a partial engine failure with two passengers on board. The only clearing within reach was a small, grass-covered sandbank on the edge of the river. He put the machine down parallel to the river. There was just room for his skids on the bank, and no more. The passengers got out while Ted ran the engine down. He switched it off and joined them for a moment to wait for the rotors to stop turning before he pulled some spark plugs to see if they had been the cause of the problem. As he stood there, the sandbank suddenly crumbled into the shallow water and the helicopter fell sideways with the blades still turning. The machine was a virtual write-off. It was a remarkable piece of ill fortune.

Ted and his passengers then had to endure a three-day walk down the rugged Homathko River to the head of Bute Inlet, where they were picked up. The wreck was soon salvaged with the help of an Okanagan helicopter, and Ted spent most of the remainder of that first year helping Ted Protheroe rebuild it.

The new company's second year of operation, 1956, was a more encouraging one. Ted went out again to the Homathko, to work with the rebuilt CF-IDX; in addition, he leased two machines, together with pilots, from Aero-Copters. The two leased machines were flown by Don Scholberg and John Watson. Meanwhile Ted hired a second engineer, Harvey Jones. They had a successful season and the future began to look rosy enough that Ted began to look for pilots to train for the following year's work.

He chose two people from different backgrounds. Robert P. Taylor was an ex-RCAF officer who had learned to fly late in the war and became an instructor. After the war he attempted to make a living as an artist, but in spite of his talent he was only just managing to survive. Early in the Korean War, he decided to rejoin the Air Force and spent the next five years training NATO students on Harvards at a training school in Calgary. By the end of five years he was becoming bored with the routine and decided he would like to fly helicopters. There were no openings in the service, so he went to see Ted Henson. Bob Taylor remembers that it was not an easy task:

"A lot of civilian operators didn't jump up and down with enthusiasm at the prospect of hiring a military pilot in those days—didn't think they would prove too useful in the bush, I guess; so we more or less had to prove otherwise. And the conversion from fixed-wing to helicopters was much harder than I had expected. For a while I didn't think I was going to make it. The training was comprehensive: we did 50 hours of basic and then another 25 hours of mountain training. Earl Thompson of Aero-Copters had already done more than 4000 hours of helicopter flying time by 1956, and in February of the next year he trained me up in Strathcona Park—Great Central Mountain and Golden Hinde were my initiation into mountain flying. It was hairy of course. You never landed far from the edge of a drop-off. You just had to hop, skip, get over the edge and clear your tail rotor and get some rpm on the way down. Terrifying."

The other pilot Ted chose was Bruce Payne. Bruce had worked in the bush, spending a summer with the B.C. Forest Service, on the Hart Highway, between Prince George and Dawson Creek, and another with the provincial Topographic Survey in northeastern British Columbia, building towers for triangulation grids. In the winters he had taken flying lessons at his own expense at the Victoria Flying Club. Ted decided to ask the club for a recommendation. Bruce, who had just turned 20, was chosen and he began his training at the same time as Bob Taylor.

*(Left) Ted Henson, on the left, and engineer Ted Protheroe. (Right) Ted Henson with Harvey Jones the day before Henson's fatal crash. (Lynn Stringer, Bob Taylor)*

In May 1957 both had completed training and were signed on as employees. An agreement had been reached that they would start at a salary of $450 a month, working up to $600 after three years, at which point their training would be considered paid for. Bob Taylor went with Ted Protheroe to the Power Commission job on the Homathko and Bruce's first revenue job was to fly people from the Department of Transport and Trans-Canada Air Lines up Mount Slesse southeast of Abbotsford, where a North Star had crashed, killing all on board.

For the rest of that season, Bruce worked on a number of jobs—some mineral exploration for Falconbridge Mining at Buggaboo Creek in the east Kootenays; powerline patrols out of Campbell River, on Vancouver Island; and a stint with the provincial Topographic Survey—before travelling all the way across to Ontario to fly a short contract with the Department of National Defence.

Meanwhile, Bob Taylor found the Homathko region an eye-opener on his first revenue flying job. He was mostly moving survey crews in preparation for dam construction. He had his first experience of slinging when he moved a big Kootenay wood-burning stove into a camp on the river. Kootenay ranges were substantial cast-iron units with double heating ovens. They were too heavy to be carried on one rack, so Bob flew his engineer to the landing site, then returned to tie the stove onto a cross-tube under the helicopter with a 10-foot length of half-inch rope.

When he reached the landing site and lowered the stove gently to the ground, the engineer, armed with a sharp knife, cut the load loose. It was an illegal and, of course, dangerous procedure. Any sort of mechanical problem en route could have been disastrous. Fortunately it was this experience that motivated Ted Protheroe to fit up part of a bomb rack from a Canso amphibian as a cargo hook, so that the load could be jettisoned in an emergency.

The third season, 1957, started out successfully for the new company. Ted Henson was quoted in an article in *Canadian Aviation:* "I started this business because I liked to fly. I've only been in it a year and yet this will have to be my last year of flying. We'll be getting a lot bigger, and managing the firm—mainly lining up work to keep the 'copters busy—will be a full-time job."

Ted spent only one short summer "flying" that managerial desk. Bruce Payne returned from his job in Ontario early in October, just as one of the Seattle pilots, whose six-month Canadian work permit had expired, was obliged to return home from the Power Commission job on the Homathko. Ted didn't have the heart to send Bruce right back out again; instead he went himself to finish the few days of work left. He was flown by floatplane into Tatlayoko Lake, a narrow body of water which stretches for some 14 miles between steep, rocky shores. The following morning, October 17, 1957, Ted took off in his helicopter for a five-minute flight along the lake to another camp. He was never seen again. The people in the camp he had just left reported hearing a heavy thud. The only remains ever found were a seat cushion and an oil can.

The loss of their president so early in the company's existence was a crushing blow. To Lynn Henson it seemed the end of so many dreams: ''The sad part was that we had to go on. I can't remember now, but I think it was two weeks before the search was called off, everything was finished and he was declared dead. But in that two-week period, every time the phone rang I thought maybe he'd walked out after all and here he was phoning. But because I'd been on the lake in the summer, and knew how treacherous it was, I couldn't really believe that. Even if he had been able to swim ashore, there was no place for him to hang on—it was just straight down and there were no little beaches for him to lie on or anything.''

The crisis was one of management and finances. The financial problem was eased by an unexpected bonus. Lynn recalls: ''When Ted and I were sitting at home, waiting for our operating licence—when Ted was still working on cars in the evenings to bring in some money—Fred McGregor, of Mutual Life, came along and sold him a $30,000 life insurance policy. Ted never told me about this. He was paying about $25 a month in premiums; and because we had so little money, he fell behind on the premiums. That was how I found out. Ted was away flying when a letter from Mutual arrived. I opened it and it said that if you don't pay by such and such a date, your insurance will no longer be in effect.

''I was pretty angry because Ted hadn't told me anything about this. I phoned Fred McGregor and told him so. I was looking after the bills and we couldn't afford it. I would find the policy and tear it up. I said, 'Thank you very much' and 'Goodbye,' and I thought that was the end of it. This was in April '57. I wasn't very nice to him. Then came October '57 and Ted was dead. And you know what happened? Mr. McGregor had been paying those premiums himself for all those months. That's what saved the company—Mr. McGregor's generosity. Without that $30,000 I would have had to sell the company to pay succession duties.''

So the financial crisis was solved, but there remained the problem of management. Lynn, who had been doing all the bookkeeping and paper work, was the only person who knew the day-to-day details of the operation. Bill Boeing called a meeting of the shareholders and the decision was reached that Lynn should be the president to run the administration of the company and that an operations manager and a chief engineer should be appointed. As the company's first employee, Ted Protheroe was obviously a candidate for the position as operations manager; but in the end Boeing recommended Bob Taylor for the job and Protheroe became chief engineer.

For Lynn, the next two years were devoted almost entirely to work in the hangar. Since she had a son who was seven and a daughter who was two, the problems were very real. She remembers the period with mixed emotions: ''That was a hard time but I had a very good baby sitter. Danny went to school and we worked things out—even though I was out at the hangar 12 hours a day every day. At the time, though, I came in for a lot of criticism from my close friends, as well as from my family. They seemed to think I should stay at home and look after my children even if that meant going on welfare.

*After Ted Henson's death, Bruce Payne, chief pilot; Lynn Henson, president; Bob Taylor, operations manager; and Harvey Jones, chief engineer, were left to carry on. (Vancouver Island Helicopters Collection)*

"Also, I found out how very quick people are to take advantage of you. One day in a grocery store I met a man who was a friend of Ted's and mine, and he wanted to buy the company. He was into another fixed-wing operation and he wanted to buy our company to amalgamate with his. I said no. He said, 'Just name your price. Every man has his price.' When I refused again he said, 'I'll give you six months to run that company into the ground!' I'm proud to think that every day that goes by makes him more wrong."

On the other side of the coin, there were considerable satisfactions for Lynn: "My office and a little room where we kept the spare parts were all we had. And my office was also the pilot and engineer crew room. That's where we all met and I tried to do my bookwork. Mind you, I loved being among them and listening to their talk about their experiences, but I was getting desperate because it was almost impossible to get any work done in that atmosphere. Then one day I remembered the story of Glen McPherson. His wife wanted a new kitchen and she kept after him and kept after him and one day she took an axe and chopped down all her cupboards. He came home from work and there was this pile of rubble in the middle of the kitchen and she was just sitting there, and she said, 'I'm not doing any cooking until I get a new kitchen.' So the next day Glen got started and had the kitchen rebuilt.

"My own solution wasn't quite so drastic. I just picked up my desk and my typewriter, went into the parts room, plunked down in the middle of the parts and said, 'I don't care what you people do; this is where I am going to work from now on!' The next day they started building a new parts room down at the back of the hangar, where it is now. The truth is I loved the work I was doing. I was determined to keep our company going for Ted's sake."

With Bob Taylor running the flying and Ted Protheroe the maintenance, business began to flourish. These were still boom years. The Power Commission work on the Homathko continued until 1959; meanwhile, Vancouver Island Helicopters was very active in mining exploration along the Stikine River in northwestern British Columbia. In January 1958, the company had on its books Bob Taylor and Bruce Payne as pilots, Ted Protheroe, Ron Adams, Howie Goodall and Harvey Jones as engineers. In February, Des O'Halloran, an ex-RCAF officer, became the company's third full-time pilot. A young Australian, Noel Dodwell, was working as a volunteer in the stock-room. In June 1959 he became an employee at a salary of $200 a month. His perseverence paid off; eventually Bob Taylor trained him as a pilot and he became a very successful one.

This was the year, too, when Bob Taylor landed the company's first B.C. Forest Service contract. Bob recalls that it was a big step forward: "It was the inventory contract, and for us it was a winner from the start. You flew nearly all the time with one passenger, so it was easy on the machine and on the pilot. You had one man on board with a tape recorder and he called what were known as plots—areas of trees perhaps half a mile long marked on aerial photographs—and the 'classifier' recorded the species, estimated heights and ages of the trees in each plot as you flew about 50 feet above them. Then, after an hour or so, we would land beside a plot right after it had been recorded and the classifier would go in and check his estimates to make sure they weren't too far out.

"What made the contract really worthwhile was that it was a big project; the inventory was to cover the whole province over a 10-year span. We had it for five years. Another good thing about it was that the forestry people would let us put a brand new pilot on the job. I'd train him in the winter, and this was an excellent job for him to build up his time without having to try anything too hairy."

Despite Bob Taylor's optimism, the inventory job could be "hairy." At least Noel Dodwell in his second year as a pilot found it so. One of the aspects of the program which Bob did not mention was the use of two-man sampling crews. These crews, almost invariably summer students, were put out by helicopter to sample random plots of trees. They would work out of a fly-camp for several days at a time, using a chain and compass to reach the randomly selected plots, and then physically measure the trees and record the data.

On this occasion, Noel had dropped the crew's food and camping gear in a clearing on the bank of a creek. Then he took off to drop the two students some three or four thousand feet up the mountain, near the tree line, so that they could put in two samples before walking back down to set up their fly-camp. He couldn't find a landing site where they wanted one and decided to prop one skid on a steep bank of scree, holding the helicopter in a semi-hover while they jumped off.

*Engineer Howie Goodall (left) and pilot Des O'Halloran freshen up KNC, north bend of Stuart Lake, 1960. (Des O'Halloran)*

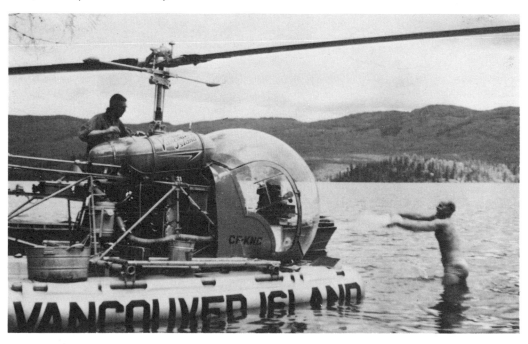

Before doing this, he explained to them the importance of leaving the helicopter one at a time, and of not lingering on the cargo rack before jumping because he could not hold the helicopter level for more than a few seconds in this unbalanced condition. Satisfied that they understood, he settled the skid on his side of the machine firmly on the scree and nodded to the student on the outside to go. Unfortunately the student was still wearing sneakers; he had tied the laces of his boots together and he was carrying them in his hand. When he got out on the rack and looked down at the jagged scree, some four or five feet beneath him, it occurred to him that he should be wearing his boots before he jumped, and he calmly sat down on the cargo rack to change into them.

Noel shouted to the student still sitting beside him to tell his companion to get the hell off the rack (or words to that effect). As the second student moved over to do so, Noel finally lost control and the helicopter rolled down the slope, thrashing itself to pieces as it did so. Astonishingly, no one suffered anything worse than minor scratches and bruises; but people in main camp, more than 10 miles away, claimed afterwards that they heard profanities couched in an Australian accent echoing among the mountain tops for several minutes.

*Most things could be tied to a helicopter, as long as they weren't too heavy. This operation in 1961 was for Noranda Mines on the west coast of Vancouver Island. H. Vernon, Noranda party chief, stands by. (Des O'Halloran)*

But this happened later, and the problems they encountered during the first three seasons were usually the result of over-eagerness to take every job that became available. As an example, in 1958 a mining exploration consulting company called J.C. Sproule and Associates, through a series of mishaps, ran out of helicopters up the Mackenzie River in the Norman Wells area. Sproule's crew were stranded in the bush for six weeks without a machine. Bob Taylor finally went up at the end of the season which, as he said, "spread the company a little thin, stretching our logistical supply line all the way from Pat Bay to Norman Wells."

Sproule had a reputation for running very economical operations, Bob recalls: "There were six of us in camp and he'd come off the plane with six steaks and six beer. That was a big, hearty surprise treat for the boys. It was at least a change from the eternal Chuckwagon stew!" [A remarkable number of the people we interviewed spoke disparagingly of Chuckwagon Dinners. Presumably the producers dealt only with exploration company purchasing agents, people who never had to go out in the bush and sample the product.]

By 1960 the operation had settled down to five machines, supplemented by as many as six leased from Aero-Copters. Most work by this time was within the province. The

Stikine River was being extensively explored—there were several large drilling projects in progress—and both provincial forestry and topographical survey contracts had been renewed. Bob Taylor became involved with experimental projects with the Forest Service: "They wanted to be able to drop food packages to people who were too far from a lake or a clearing to be reached," Bob recalls. "These packages weighed about 30 or 40 pounds each. We tried free-dropping them, but that didn't work very well—too many of them ended up smashed on the rocks. So we came up with the idea of attaching small parachutes to the packages, hooking them on to a bomb rack—we must have cornered the market on surplus Canso bomb racks—and tying the static lines to the cargo racks. Then all we had to do was to punch off the packages and the parachute would be yanked open automatically by the static cord. Trouble was, we had the packages on a short cord, hooked onto the bomb rack, and we hadn't figured out that the airstream would twist the loads round and round.

"The first time I tried it, I had two of these packages hooked up. They obviously began to twist as soon as we took off. Just before I reached the drop area, one of the 'chutes opened by itself—the package had twisted until the static line tightened up enough to open it. So there we were all of a sudden, with the nose going down and when I looked back the 'chute was open and oscillating right by the tail rotor. I was afraid to punch it off in case it wrapped itself around the tail rotor. And I didn't want to let down too quickly for the same reason. The problem was to keep the nose up; I had the cyclic [stick] right back in my stomach. I tell you, there were two guys compressing their backs against the firewall. In the end, I sort of sideslipped and punched off both packages. The guys on the ground thought it was a big joke. They thanked me for waiting until I got close enough for them to retrieve the packages."

This was one of several experiments conducted by the Forest Service with helicopters. Another successful one in which Bob Taylor was involved was the use of a camera boom for stereoscopic aerial photography. At first the boom was attached under the frame of the helicopter; later it was slung from the cargo hook. The boom, which was about 12 feet long, had two cameras mounted on it, one at either end. The cameras were operated electrically, by remote control, from inside the helicopter. This made it possible to cover the ground with overlapping photographs which, when fed into a stereoscopic plotting machine, made it possible to measure the heights of the trees very accurately. Using colour photography, the species and ages of the trees could also be estimated with some precision. In the end, this system permitted forest inventory to be conducted without the need for a classifier in the helicopter—a saving, both in time and manpower.

Some years later Bruce Payne took off with the test version of the camera boom slung on the cargo hook. He was flying a turbine-powered Alouette, a much faster machine than the Bell, and the purpose was to test the boom for high-altitude photography at 115 knots. As it turned out, this was fast enough to induce the camera to fly on its own. The boom came up and thumped the bottom of the helicopter; fortunately no serious damage was done and the boom was then modified so that it could be clamped to the bottom of the helicopter.

Another, more conventional job Bob remembers with a faint shudder was the installation of a Pacific Great Eastern (B.C. Railway) micro-wave tower: "If you look up the side of Lillooet Mountain, you'll see that it was pretty hairy. The sidehill is just about vertical. They blasted a little 14-foot by 14-foot pad off the top of a shoulder and it was a straight drop of 3000 feet down to the valley floor—I mean straight down. They lost a couple of pack horses getting up there to blast the pad.

"When you landed there, you had to be careful about stepping out because there was practically no place to stand. And the winds you'd get were unreal; you'd toss a

*Versions of the 70mm camera boom resembled something more appropriate to science fiction than forestry. (British Columbia Ministry of Forests)*

piece of plywood or something over the side and it would come spitting back up at you. The pad was on the northeast side, so you nearly always had subsiding air. You hardly ever got an updraft to help you get the tower steel up there; you had to dog it all the way up. And sometimes, when you got there, you'd get all set up on your approach and then at the last minute suddenly lose 200 feet and have to start all over again. We went through eight pilots on that job. Some of them would just take one look at it and catch the next PGE train out.''

While these things were happening, a meeting which had taken place shortly after Ted Henson's death was to have a good deal of influence on the future of Vancouver Island Helicopters. The company had carried a life insurance policy on Ted and when it was paid, they used the premium to purchase a new helicopter in 1958—a Bell 47-G2, registered CF-KNC. By the time the machine arrived in Victoria, however, it was so late in the season that Lynn could not place it on a contract. Rather than leave it sitting in the hangar for the rest of the summer, Lynn offered it on lease to Okanagan. She and Bob Taylor went across to Vancouver to discuss the details with Alf Stringer, Okanagan's operations manager.

"It was a very business-like meeting," Lynn recalls. "We made the necessary arrangements for the lease and then left. But later, in 1959, there was a celebration of 50 years of flight in Canada, and I received an invitation to attend the banquet at a Vancouver hotel with Alf Stringer. I was very flattered that this important man from Okanagan would invite me. And it was an exciting evening: Igor Sikorsky was there as one of the guest speakers, so I met him, too. Anyway, the eventual result of that meeting was that Alf and I were married the next year and I went to live in Vancouver for the next three years.''

Six months after her second marriage, and just before the move to Vancouver, Lynn suffered another tragedy. Her 10-year-old son was struck down and killed by a truck in Gordon Head. However, life had to go on and she moved to a large house which she and Alf had had built in the Oak Ridge area of Vancouver.

For the next three years, she ran VIH largely by phone. Then, because Carl Agar's health had broken down and he had retired from Okanagan, and because Alf was finding himself increasingly at odds with management, Alf decided to resign. "It was," as Lynn observes, "an awful wrench for him. He had built up this little company until it was one of the biggest helicopter companies in the world. So it was quite a letdown for him to come and operate five helicopters after being operations manager for Okanagan.''

Alf Stringer became president of VIH and Lynn, as she puts it, "stepped out of the picture and stayed home and had children." As it turned out, Alf's first few years with VIH were not easy. The early and middle sixties were recession years and profits were scant. But gradually he built the company up to a 12-machine operation, and his helicopters were so meticulously maintained that they were always a source of pride to their crews. After an experiment with an Alouette III, which turned out to be uneconomical for the small jobs and too small for the heavy-lift work, the company was equipped with turbine-powered Bell 206 Jet Rangers. It still operates from the same hangar at Victoria International today.

*Vancouver Island Helicopters used an Alouette III similar to this Bullock Helicopters machine seen about to land on the Bugaboo Glacier. (Tourism B.C.)*

# CHAPTER 5

# Okanagan: One of the Largest Helicopter Operators in the World

*A number of us decided that, instead of sitting at home, licking our wounds, we should bloody well do something. So we said to the company, "Give us a machine and we'll go out and try to get some work for it."*

DON MACKENZIE

For Okanagan Helicopters, 1952 marked the change from individual to corporate management. Not only did bookkeeper Frances Heron move from Kelowna to join Ada Carlson as the second woman employee, but there was a significant change in management. The board of directors resolved that Carl Agar was carrying too heavy an administrative and executive burden. Consequently, Glen McPherson became executive vice-president and treasurer, to assume responsibility for marketing and finance, leaving Carl Agar free to look after the operational and training functions of the business.

This move had been necessary because the number of enquiries for technical assistance and advice facing Okanagan, particularly from the military, was becoming unmanageable. A major from the United States Marine Corps was more or less seconded to the company, sitting in at virtually all its meetings except board meetings. The new administration began what was to be an era of amalgamations and the formation of numerous subsidiaries to deal with the growing complexity of their operations.

The first of these subsidiaries was called Sintilopter Surveys Ltd. Formed in conjunction with Warmac Exploration Ltd., it was to provide airborne geiger and scintillometer surveys for geological exploration companies searching for radioactive minerals. At the same time, Agar Helicopter Consultants Ltd. was set up to deal with the ever-increasing volume of enquiries about helicopter operations. Carl became an advisor to both the Canadian and the United States military—but now the company was getting paid for his services.

By 1953 the company was beginning to get its financial head above the water, and it took up its option to purchase one of the Alcan S-55s for $115,000. Operating profits had risen to $93,000 and towards the end of the year the company formed a much larger subsidiary. J.C. "Jack" Charleson of Ottawa, who had worked in aviation for the federal government and private industry, and who was one of Canada's first licensed helicopter pilots, became president of the new company, United Helicopters Ltd., formed to serve eastern Canada. One of its first tasks was to provide services to the federal government and the provincial fisheries department in Newfoundland.

In 1954 there were signs of healthy growth. A contract was awarded to Dominion Construction Ltd. to build a new 10,000-square-foot hangar, together with 5000 square feet of office space at Vancouver International Airport. But 1955 was the year of expansion. Okanagan took over and incorporated into United Helicopters, the major part of the flying assets of Kenting Helicopters Ltd. and Smart Aviation Ltd., most of which had previously been owned by the Abitibi Power and Paper Company. Alf Stringer was appointed general man-

*(Left) In 1952 Okanagan underwent a profound change in personnel, corporate structure and, before long, aircraft. Central to these was president Glen McPherson, shown on the left with Alf Stringer and Carl Agar. They appear to be contemplating the state of the company's finances. (Right) Jack Charleson became president of a major Okanagan subsidiary, United Helicopters, formed to serve eastern Canadian customers. Charleson was one of the first Canadians to fly helicopters. (Gordy Askin, Milberry Collection)*

ager of this enlarged subsidiary and moved to Toronto to take up his responsibilities.

Also, one of the first and largest of the Geological Survey of Canada helicopter operations took place in 1955. Called the "Franklin Project," it was to be "a broad geological survey of the Arctic Islands, of the Franklin District, Northwest Territories, the major part of Queen Elizabeth Islands and northern parts of Somerset and Prince of Wales Islands, plus the northwest part of Baffin Island."

This was an ambitious project, lasting from June to September. Two of Okanagan's S-55's CF-HHU and CF-HVR, were fitted with improved radio equipment and directional gyro-compasses. Then they were transported from Toronto to Resolute Bay, N.W.T., in an RCAF C-119. Fred Snell was in charge of the Okanagan crew, George Chamberlain the supervising engineer. Orr, Iverson and Hazell were the other pilots; Kelly, Grover and Bryant the engineers. The party chief was Dr. Y.O. Foutier and Dr. E.F. Roots was controller of aircraft movements. In addition, there were nine geologists, nine assistant geologists, and two cooks. A successful enterprise, this was the forerunner of many other Geological Survey of Canada helicopter operations.

There was much else going on in 1955. The company worked on a forest inventory survey between Kitimat and Prince Rupert; a Shell Oil geological survey in the Fort Simpson area and the Mackenzie Basin; and an extensive aerial survey for Northwest Explorations Ltd. in the Watson Lake area, on the British Columbia-Yukon border. All of this was in addition to smaller prospecting, freighting and power line patrol operations, as well as an emergency two-machine operation in Kildala Pass, where Alcan's power transmission line had been knocked out by a snowslide.

By the end of 1955, the company employed 90 people, its helicopters had logged 12,000 hours of revenue flying, and gross revenue had grown from $740,000 the previous year to

*Okanagan S-55s used on Project Franklin were flown north to Resolute in RCAF C-119s. Operating conditions required the addition of improved radio equipment and gyro compasses to the helicopters; magnetic compasses would have been useless that close to the north magnetic pole. (Alf Stringer)*

*Eric Cowden, like many in the helicopter industry in British Columbia, got his start in aviation with Queen Charlotte Airlines. (Eric Cowden)*

$1,555,000—for a profit of $127,000. But perhaps the most significant news was that negotiations were progressing with the federal government for a contract to provide helicopter contruction and maintenance services on the Mid-Canada Line. The government was considering the purchase of 20 S-55s by the RCAF, all of which would be turned over to Okanagan to operate on a cost-plus basis. The Mid-Canada Line was an aircraft surveillance radar line between Dawson Creek, British Columbia, and Hopedale, Labrador. The helicopters were to be based at Dawson Creek, Fort MacMurray, Cranberry Portage, Bird, Winisk, Great Whale River and Knob Lake (Schefferville). Once construction of the line was completed in 1956, three helicopters would be stationed at each base to carry out maintenance and re-supply of the intermediate sites, with the exception of Dawson Creek, which would have two.

Construction of the Line was being carried out by the RCAF, using H-19s, H-34s and H-21s. Okanagan began work with two S-55s on the Line to help with construction before it was completed. Eric Cowden recalls arriving in Fort MacMurray with his pilot, Murray Couch, in 1956. When they stepped out of the helicopter, they were asked when the rest of their crew would be joining them. Eric replied that he and Murray were the crew! The RCAF were used to working with five or six crew members for each helicopter.

The Mid-Canada Line promised the same benefits as the Alcan contract—it would be a year-round operation, and it should be possible to plan for several years ahead. However, by the time the maintenance contract was finally awarded, competitors were in the field. Okanagan's hopes of winning the entire contract faded when Spartan Air Services of Ottawa was given the eastern section of the Line between James Bay and Labrador. Spartan was equipped with RCAF-owned Vertol 42s and 44s (the civil designation for the H-21 "flying banana").

Although the Mid-Canada was a desirable operation for management, for the crews working on it there were some singular disadvantages. Their responsibility was to provide the sites with food, mail, supplies, fuel oil for the electrical generators, as well as the electronic and mechanical maintenance technicians when they were required. The radar sites were located some 20 miles apart, and flying from one to the other became much like truck driving. Each site had a prepared landing pad and after the initial familiarization, there were few challenges.

The main challenge, as it turned out, was posed by the fact that the line was obsolete before it was even completed. This meant that few were inclined to take their jobs seriously; an attitude of indifference prevailed amongst the crews whose responsibility it was to maintain the equipment on each site. For example, each site had a small Petter diesel engine running the generator, which in turn ran the electrically operated avgas pumps. In

*The Bell 47-B3s in the Okanagan fleet were kept in operation long after introduction of later models. The original Okanagan B3, CF-FZX, in greatly altered form, is shown here receiving floats. (Alf Stringer)*

*An Okanagan S-55 at Toronto Island, April 1959. (K.M. Molson)*

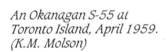

winter, Okanagan's crews spent more time working on these diesels than they did on the helicopters.

But what seems to have frustrated the crews most was the failure of ground crew to prepare a load in time for an early morning takeoff during the winter. If the helicopter crew could get away at a reasonable hour, say 8:30, they could fly to the end of their section of the line and back before darkness fell at about four o'clock in the afternoon. When in base, the helicopters were stored in a heated hangar. If they had to stay out on one of the sites, the problems of starting in the morning were compounded by the lack of ongoing maintenance. The gas-driven heaters would seldom start; and when they did, it took a long time to warm things up sufficiently to start the helicopter and clean the accumulated ice and snow off the machine. All the crews accepted the inevitability of these disagreeable exigencies in winter operations. However, when problems were unnecessary, they caused a good deal of friction.

The results for the company, though, were significant. By late 1956, Okanagan was operating three S-58s, 13 S-55s (10 RCAF, 3 their own) and 22 Bell 47s—nearly all the latter by now converted to G-2s with the more powerful Lycoming engine—for a total of 35 machines. The staff had increased to 108 and they were one of the largest helicopter companies in the world.

But there were disconcerting clouds on the horizon. Competition was increasing. In 1954, as we have seen, Vancouver Island Helicopters was granted an operating licence in spite of strenuous opposition from Okanagan. Then, towards the end of 1955, Pacific Western Airlines, run by one of the old-time bush pilots, Russ Baker, decided to get into the helicopter business. Bill McLeod recalls that it was not difficult for him to make the decision to move from Okanagan: "Not only did it offer more money, but it was an opportunity to sort of create something myself. Back in the days when I had first come over to the mainland from Vancouver Island and I was going through ground school with the Brisbane company, I shared a room with a guy called Laidman, Dick Laidman. He was with PWA. He got hold of me and said they wanted to form a helicopter division—would I be interested in setting it up and managing it? They made me an offer I just couldn't refuse and I joined them."

PWA's helicopter division started with one Bell 47-G1. By the end of the year it had bought five more. At its peak it was operating 12 machines—six owned and six leased. It succeeded in winning all the forestry contracts available and did all the helicopter work on the Bennett dam project on the Peace River. But PWA had over-extended itself. It had bought and leased a number of large fixed-wing aircraft for work on the DEW Line in the Arctic, and since it was funded to a large extent by the Federal Development Bank, PWA was obliged to rationalize operations. The bank gave PWA an ultimatum: either become an airline or return to being a bush operator. It decided to become an airline and sold all fixed-wing bush operations as well as the helicopter division.

The helicopter operation was bought by a group headed by Jim Storey, an ex-Trans-Canada Air Lines captain, and the name was simply changed to Pacific Helicopters Ltd. Under its new management, the company continued to compete with Okanagan until 1959, when Okanagan bought all its assets and equipment. Though buying out the opposition was an effective solution, this was an option not always available. When John Diefenbaker's Conservative government came into power in 1957, the newly appointed Minister of Transport, George Hees, adopted a policy of *laissez faire* in commercial aviation, and Okanagan complained, with considerable justification, that it was now possible for newly-formed companies to bid on government contracts, and often win them, before they even had any machines or hired any crews.

What Okanagan was complaining about was the ultimate in free enterprise, but it had some singular disadvantages, both for the customer and the operator. One-machine com-

*Pacific Western Helicopter Division operated this Bell Model 47-H, one of the few helicopters of the type used in British Columbia. It was a "tarted up" version of the Bell 47-G2 for the executive market. (British Columbia Ministry of Forests)*

panies did sometimes give good service, but more often they suffered an accident and, without any back-up in spares or expertise, often folded and disappeared for good. There was also the question of safety. The most expensive part of a helicopter operation is maintenance. It was an ever-present temptation for a small company to skimp on maintenance, and try to operate with marginally qualified crews. For an established company like Okanagan it was bound to be galling to be deprived of business by people with little operating experience, and by 1959 the strain was beginning to show. That year they suffered their first retrenchment, selling United Helicopters to Eastern Provincial Airlines. Brief statistics for the years 1957 to 1959 give some indication of the problems. Although the size of the fleet was increasing, profits were not:

| YEAR | REVENUE | NET PROFIT | AIRCRAFT | HOURS |
|------|---------|------------|----------|-------|
| 1957 | $2,888,115 | $312,568 | 47 | 22,000 |
| 1958 | $3,188,382 | $254,412 | 54 | 24,000 |
| 1959 | $3,044,004 | $282,659 | 57 | 26,000 |

Several new companies sprang up to provide competition in British Columbia in the '50s. In addition to Vancouver Island and PWA, Highland Helicopters, Haida Helicopters and some one-machine companies began operating. On top of this, there was incursion from companies based in Alberta, particularly Foothills Helicopters and Alpine Helicopters. Okanagan's principal complaint was that at least some of the companies had an unfair advantage. It pointed out that because these companies were under-staffed and had little or no back-up equipment, which meant low overhead, they could easily underbid Okanagan.

*A helicopter service connecting Victoria and Vancouver, the major population centres of British Columbia, has often been proposed since 1945. One of the most ambitious plans was for the introduction of the Fairey Rotodyne, a British-design combining features of both fixed- and rotary-wing aircraft. Carl Agar and Alf Stringer went to the UK to view the prototype. The Rotodyne was unsuccessful and never got beyond the experimental stage. Proposals to build the aircraft in the Victoria Fairey plant likewise fell through. (Alf Stringer)*

*A Sikorsky S-62 demonstrator landing in Victoria Harbour, early 1960s. (Bill Halkett)*

There was some merit in the argument and unfortunately private industry and government alike were inclined to accept the lowest bid without question.

But by the end of the decade a worse problem seemed to be the growing tension between individuals in management. The most contentious issue was diversification of the fleet. Until then, the company had operated only Bell 47s as their light machines and Sikorsky S-55s for heavier work. A decision was made to introduce the Hiller 12E, a machine comparable to the Bell 47-G2. Those who disagreed claimed there were two potential disadvantages: first, it would mean two sets of spare parts and special tools; second, the Bell had proved itself operationally with Okanagan, but the Hiller hadn't. The result, the dissenters were quick to point out, proved to be an expensive mistake. There was a problem with the balancing of the crankshaft and the engine mounts in the 12E. This led to what were described as harmonic vibrations—a condition which caused long-term maintenance problems, and cost the company lost revenue flying time.

A similar problem arose in connection with a contract awarded by the United States government to operated two machines from Goose Bay, Labrador. In addition to an S-58, management decided to buy a Sikorsky S-62, a machine which turned out to be unsuitable for the operation, just as some in Okanagan had predicted. Other controversial projects were initiated at this time: announcements were made in the media that Okanagan had placed an option on the British Fairey Rotodyne, a composite helicopter/fixed-wing aircraft with a capacity for 70 passengers and a top speed of 200 mph. It was to be used on a scheduled service between Vancouver and Victoria. But the Rotodyne was still experimental and never did fly commercially. This was followed by the setting up of another subsidiary, Copter Cabs, to provide commuter service for the Greater Vancouver area, using three-passenger Bell 47-Js. This venture was a financial failure.

Meantime, the company continued to grow during the last years of the decade. A constant stream of Canadian, U.S. and overseas trainees passed through Bud Tillotson's mountain training school in Penticton. Then, in 1958, the company was awarded a contract by the Southern California Edison Company to construct a power transmission line through the Soledad Canyon, northeast of Los Angeles. Concrete bases were poured by an S-58, then pre-rigged wooden poles were dropped into the prepared sockets in the concrete. The operation was a success and was widely reported in North America.

Also about this time, one of the directors decided it was time to have the story of the company written for publication in book form. As Barney Bent describes it: ''The board agreed to have an acquaintance of one of the directors carry out this work on a retainer fee of $400 a month, plus expenses, to a maximum of $4000. After the financial and time limits had been exceeded (the writer had moved in with the Agars to be close to detailed information, and refreshment), he gave up and left for parts unknown.''

Now, the company's story was entering a period of dissention. By 1960, Carl Agar's health had begun to deteriorate; he had emphysema. Unfortunately, this illness coincided with growing conflict between some of the directors. The following year, disaffected but no longer strong enough to put up a fight, Carl submitted a letter of resignation to the board. At a meeting called by the directors, which must have been an unusually tense occasion, Alf Stringer presented a forthright criticism of a number of managerial decisions to which both he and Carl Agar had been opposed. Glen McPherson, the president, offered to resign. However, further discussion produced a compromise. Carl Agar would take a three-month leave of absence; both Glen McPherson and Alf Stringer, who had also been contemplating resignation, would stay on while a firm of management consultants, Douglas Dewar's old company, Peat, Marwick, Mitchell, conducted a management study and made recommendations for the future.

In the end, the consultant's report had little effect, and both Carl and Alf resigned in

*Bud Tillotson, on the left in the photo above, ran Okanagan's mountain training program, a demanding task which greatly enhanced the reputation of the company. Students from all over the world learned how, in the lyrical prose of a Bell publication, to read the "subtle, quiet (and potentially treacherous) language of mountain air . . . feeling the subtleties of its 'bad air' (downdrafts) and 'good air' (power for free, upmoving)." (Bell Helicopters Textron)*

*Okanagan purchased helicopters of greater capacity such as this Sikorsky S-58 as they became available, buying the first of the type used in Canada in 1956. These machines were quickly put to work setting power poles in the Quesnel area and in California, where they received considerable publicity. (Okanagan Helicopters Collection)*

Don MacKenzie (right) and an employee of the Kootenay Power Commission near the Lower Arrow Dam, Castlegar, circa 1963. MacKenzie, now Okanagan's chief pilot, earned the Helicopter Association of America's "Pilot of the Year Award" in 1971. He landed a badly disabled S-61 on an oil rig off Nova Scotia, saving the lives of 16 passengers and crew. In 1983 he was involved in the development of Emergency Multi-Person Rescue Apparatus (EMPRA) which will, if adopted, greatly increase the speed with which hoist rescues can be made. (Okanagan Helicopters Collection)

1963, Carl to go into retirement until 1966, when he rejoined Okanagan as a board member and consultant until his death in 1968, and Alf to take over management of Vancouver Island Helicopters from his wife, Lynn. It was a sad day for Okanagan Helicopters, complicated by the economy swinging from the boom of the '50s to the recession of the early '60s. The company recorded an operating loss of $171,000 in 1962, and for the first time operational crews were laid off during the winter months.

Don MacKenzie, later chief pilot for the company, recalls those difficult years. He had been a co-pilot with Canadian Pacific Airlines before joining Okanagan in 1960. Ironically, he had left the airline because he was looking for more security: "As a co-pilot in CPA I started out at $300 a month and worked up to $700. In fact, the captains' deductions were bigger than my pay cheque. That was the rule of thumb then. I joined Okanagan because a number of my very close friends were with them at the time, fellows like Don Poole and Jim Grady, and they persuaded me that helicopters had only been around a few years and were obviously the coming thing. That, plus the insecurity in the airlines at the time—there were a lot of lay-offs, a lot of moves back and forth—made me think this would be the right move."

As it turned out, Don experienced the classic example of "out of the frying pan into the fire." Two years later he was faced with the lay-off problem again: "That was a tough year, 1962. We had our very first lay-offs. And the first guys in from the bush at the end of the summer got laid off. We all tried to jockey for position. I think it was the only year in memory when people actually tried to stay out in the bush."

Curiously, it was the pilots rather than management who proposed a solution and pointed the way to the future. In spite of anxiety, Don remembers it as a challenging and satisfying period: "A number of us decided that, instead of sitting at home, licking our wounds, we should bloody well do something. So we said to the company, 'Give us a machine and we'll go out and try to get some work for it.' Glen McPherson, the president, was apprehensive at first, but eventually he agreed and I took a machine and went up to Squamish and worked out of a resort called Paradise Valley, flying skiers to Diamond Head and Whistler, doing a little hydro work, and occasional trips for Highways and B.C. Rail—that sort of thing. It tided us over the winter months. Then the next year I joined Jim Grady who had started a base in Nelson the year before.''

The idea of bases caught on quickly and before long Okanagan had them spotted across British Columbia. Nearly all the bases became self-supporting during winter and made money during the rest of the year. By 1968 management had changed. Ian Kennedy became president for two years, and in 1970 John Pitts replaced him. The company moved into larger machines, Sikorsky S-61s, and began to expand into overseas markets. The first of these operations was a short-lived contract using two S-61s to service off-shore oil rigs in the North Sea.

Because of time constraints, the decision was made to fly the first machine to Britain rather than ship it by sea, as had been the case with previous overseas contracts. This was historic flight, the first unescorted crossing of the Atlantic by a helicopter. The machine was flown by Russ Lennox, a Sikorsky company pilot, and Okanagan's Tommy Scheer. Keith Rutledge was the engineer. The route followed was from the Sikorsky plant in Bridgeport, up through Quebec to Baffin Island. From there they crossed Davis Strait from Cape Dyer to Søndrestrøm in Greenland, over the ice cap, and across Denmark Strait to Reykjavik, Iceland, then down through the Faroes to the British Isles. It was a route they were to follow a number of times in the future. In 1973, chief pilot Don Jacques and his crew flew an S-61 all the way from Canada to Britain, across Europe, the Middle-East and most of Asia to Songkhla in Thailand—a distance of 12,650 miles. The S-61 was a remarkable improvement over the little Bell 47-B3 Carl Agar had flown only 25 years earlier.

*Helicopters Underslung Sprayers (HUSS) Buckets were a successful British Columbia innovation. Empty buckets are simply exchanged for ones that are filled. This minimizes turnaround time. This HUSS bucket is attached to the cargo hook of an Okanagan Hiller 12-E. (Okanagan Helicopters Collection)*

# Life in the Bush I

*No bread, no vegetables, no meat. I didn't quite have*
*scurvy, but I was awfully close to it. My gums were all sore*
*and I had lost 36 pounds.*

IAN DUNCAN

Perhaps because people needed relief from the starkness of the industrial revolution, society invested flying with an aura of glamour and romance from its very beginnings. The First World War helped entrench the profession with an almost mediaeval romanticism: pilots became individual knights, jousting in chargers of wood and doped fabric. The words chivalry and gallantry became unavoidable in any description of the war in the air. Canadians had more than their fair share of heroes: Billy Bishop, Raymond Collishaw, Billy Barker, Don MacLaren—indeed the great Red Baron himself was finally shot down by a Canadian: Roy Brown.

This romanticism carried into the bush flying era. Canadian bush pilots became a symbol of individual bravery. Alone, they challenged what have been described as "the magnificent distances." As fixed-wing flying became more organized and moved into the realm of large corporations, some of the glamour began to fade. It was somewhat revived when helicopter pilots appeared on the scene, challenging nature in their frail, fluttering machines. For the helicopter pilots, though, as for the earlier generation of bush pilots, the supposed glamour and romance carried a penalty. It provided the businessmen who employed pilots with a neat rationalization: Since pilots were enjoying emotional benefits not available to others, they did not need the reward of appropriate financial benefits.

This fact became very obvious in Kemano, when a little ripple of scandal was provoked by the discovery that the helicopter crews were earning, by a considerable margin, the lowest salaries on the project. Even the most unskilled ditch-digger received a larger pay cheque. It left a bad taste in the mouth—but not bad enough to provoke any immediate remedies.

At least on the Kemano project the helicopter crews were well fed and housed. When they began to move out into other projects—into mining exploration and survey operations in the bush—they were to discover another drawback to their newly adopted profession. It revolved around what Alvin Toffler a few years later was to describe as "future shock". Customers who hired a helicopter on contract were literally shocked at the cost. Although one part of them knew that they were now able to cover ten times the area and accomplish in one season what would have taken at least five seasons by the conventional means—pack horses and back-packing—still they were appalled by the $100-an-hour rate for a helicopter. So they quickly persuaded themselves that they would have to compensate by cutting their food, accommodation and supplies budget to the bare bones.

For the crews, this meant tiny, worn-out tents and little or no fresh food. Fixed-wing re-supply trips were kept to a minimum, which meant that crews seldom received mail or news of the outside. Ironically, the technical progress represented by the helicopter had jumped the bush crews back at least 50 years. Nowhere did these economies manifest themselves more clearly than in the provisions made for the helicopter crews. They were, almost invariably, the last people to arrive in a bush camp. As they flew over it for the first time, they would usually see one tattered pup-tent pitched some distance from the other tents, and they

*A helicopter would bring in the materials to construct a camp and even its own pad. Trees have been topped to permit a safe approach to this pad. (British Columbia Ministry of Forests)*

would say to each other, ''I bet that's ours!'' Alas, they were usually right.

Eric Cowden, an engineer with Okanagan Helicopters (later with Vancouver Island Helicopters), describes what it was like to go out on an operation in those early days. He too had made the transition from Queen Charlotte Airlines to helicopters; in fact, he had just completed his training period under Alf Stringer. His pilot was Don Poole, and they set off from Vancouver for Stewart in the spring of 1953. Before they reached the bush camp, however, and faced the discouraging conditions, they had other problems. Fuel caches were few and far between along the coast, so they always carried at least four five-gallon cans of avgas on the racks. On this occasion, the leg from Prince Rupert to Stewart was a critical one, as a stiff northwest wind was blowing:

''We got into Rupert and over-nighted there'', Eric recalls. ''Next morning we headed up to Stewart. There was a terrific outflow (wind) that day. We'd already landed on the American side, which we weren't supposed to do—but you had to gas up somewhere. After we'd put the four fives into the tank, we set off up the Portland Canal. We were going nowhere —you know what it's like on floats: about 20 miles an hour. And it was one of those days—a low overcast, so you couldn't climb out of the Canal and land up top somewhere. There wasn't even a boat around . . . nothing.

''Finally Don said to me, 'What do you think?' I said, 'Well, Don, my watch says we're not going to make it.' 'You know what?' he replied. 'So does mine.'

''Anyway, there was no place to land, so we just had to keep on chugging up the Canal, doing a little praying. Finally, we turned a corner and got some shelter from the wind. When we reached Stewart, I drained the tank. We had two gallons left—enough for about six or seven more minutes of flying.''

The job Don Poole and Eric Cowden were to do in Stewart was supposed to last 10 days, after which they were to return to Vancouver; instead, they stayed out for five and a half months. To begin with, they were flying between Stewart and the Granduc Glacier. This was the site of the Granduc Copper Mine, which has suffered various reversals of fortune, closing down and then re-opening several times over the years. When they had finished there, they were sent to another mining exploration job, and, as Eric recalls, things started to go downhill:

''From Stewart we went to Bobquin Lake with two geologist—McKenzie and Warren were their names, two guys who believed in living on bacon, bannock and beans. With a little tea and sugar, that's about all they had in their so-called camp. For several weeks we worked out of a little island in the middle of Bobquin. We stayed there about five weeks, and I'll never laugh again when people make jokes about beans.

''From there we moved to Hottah Lake and then to Chukachida, more or less in the middle of the province. We were with some hot-shot mining promoter now—I remember this guy very well; I guess he was worth lots of money and behaved accordingly. The first

*Maintenance in the bush often meant pressing into service materials readily at hand. Trees would be cut, stripped of their branches and rigged into an A-frame for a hoist to remove a rotor or engine. (Okanagan Helicopters Collection)*

*In cold frosty weather, as much of the helicopter as possible was covered at night. Here the engine and transmission are still enclosed and the nylon covers are being removed from the blades of the main rotor. (Bob Taylor)*

day we were there he came into the camp, in a beat-up old Travelair flown by Doug Chappelle, and the next morning the weather was socked in tight, right down on the deck. I heard him say to the party chief, George Radisics, 'What's the weather like, George?' And George said, 'It's socked in tight—but I think it'll clear up by noon.' The promoter said, 'That's not good enough. *I* want it clear *now*!' I guess he thought he could buy the weather, too.''

This was just a beginning. Eric had other problems. The fixed-wing aircraft used on that operation, a venerable Travelair, was in sad condition. The company operating it had not provided a licensed engineer, so Eric found that he was expected to inspect it and sign the log book when it was due for a 100-hour maintenance check. Every time the Travelair, which of course was on floats, had been pulled up onto the beach to be loaded or unloaded, Eric had heard what he described as a funny noise. When the time came for the inspection and signature, he got somebody to grab the tail section and rock the machine up and down.

Sure enough, one of the mounts on the struts which connected the floats to the fuselage was just about ready to fall off. Eric refused to sign the log until the aircraft had been repaired —something that could not be done in the bush—and was exposed to ferocious recriminations from the mining promoter. In the end, everybody took off in the Travelair for Prince George, leaving Don and Eric sitting alone in camp for three days.

Their next move was to Yehinika Lake, a little to the southwest of Telegraph Creek. This was still Eric's first season in the bush, and his helicopter, CF-ETQ, even though it was a brand new Bell 47-D1, gave trouble: ''We'd been having the usual snags with those old Franklin engines. They were very hard on plugs—we were constantly having to change plugs and dig the lead out of the electrodes; and the fan belts kept letting go. When they did, they'd smack into the back of the firewall, scaring hell out of the pilot . . . and then he'd have to get down on the ground within a couple of minutes and shut down or the engine would over-heat.

''Those were routine problems, but this engine began to give me much more than that —nothing but grief. I thought the timing of the magnetos was out. Trouble was, I didn't have a manual with me on that trip. And this was a 200-horsepower engine. I'd been working on a 170-horsepower one, so I didn't really know what the timing should be. I thought I remembered Sig (Hubenig) say it was 36 degrees—so I retimed the whole thing. It didn't do a damned bit of good. Yehinika Lake was well up in the mountains and we still had a very rough engine. I checked the plugs and the points—re-set the gap—and everything was as it should be. Had me baffled there for a while; then, when I was shutting down—I shut down with the mixture control—and just before the engine quit, it suddenly smoothed out.

''So I fired up again and played with the mixture—we had a manual mixture control in those days. It would run fine just before it quit. I came to the conclusion it just had to be the carburetor. Trouble was I had never taken one apart before. I pulled the carb off the intake and split it—and out fell a little ball check-valve. It was a bad scene because I hadn't the faintest idea where it had come from. I thought, 'Oh, my God! Here we are, way out in the tules and our only way to get out is in that damned helicopter.'

''Anyway, I found the float level was way out—way beyond limits, so I set that all up. Now I really had to decide where this little ball had to go. In the end, the only place that looked likely was the accelerator-pump deal; so I popped it in there, clamped the carburetor together and bolted it back onto the manifold. When I fired up the engine, it ran like a charm. I didn't bother telling Don about the worry-session with the check-valve. When he got back from a quick test flight and thanked me because the engine was running good, I just shrugged and said, 'That's what I'm here for.' ''

In truth, the helicopter engineer did a good deal of worrying at that time. Confidence, in both machine and pilot, was to come with experience. Few of the bush camps had radio and, in any case, geologists were always secretive; they did not want people to know where they were. Thus Don Poole would leave camp early in the morning with a couple of geologists, cheerfully advising Eric that he would be back in three or four hours. Then began the long wait. Geologists, if they think they may be on to something significant, lose all track of time. Eric remembers this only too clearly: "Noon would go by; supper time would go by, and still no helicopter. And I'm pacing up and down—I tell you, I had trail worn down along that shoreline that was knee-deep, pacing up and down, worrying; what am I going to do? I'm in camp all alone, no radio in those days, or anything. And then, just as it was beginning to get dark, you'd hear it. I could hear a helicopter 30 miles away. Talk about worry; man alive!"

This same theme of anxiety was reflected by Ian Duncan, another pioneer Okanagan company engineer, later with the Canadian Coast Guard. He remembers when they were working for the Canadian Army, doing barometer surveys out of Puntzi Lake, some 50 miles west of the town of Williams Lake: "About a week after we'd arrived there, the pilot, Mike (McDonagh), took off with this lieutenant and his barometer and all his instruments and away they went. 'Be gone four hours, Duncan,' he said. I said, 'Okay, fine.' So four hours went by, and then five hours, and I started to get up off my cot in the tent; I started to walk around the tent. By the time it got dark, I had worn a trench about two feet deep around the tent—just walking around, you know. Believe me, you worry a lot when you don't know what's happened. Finally, just after breakfast next morning, in comes the pilot, back to camp. He'd walked all night, and you could see the blisters on his feet; his feet were bleeding."

Apparently Mike had tried to pull up too sharply after taking off from a little sand beach. He lost his revs and, since his machine was not on floats, it just settled into the water. Ian Duncan got hold of a 4-wheel-drive Dodge Powerwagon from the Army and made good use of the winch on the front of it, hauling himself through several swamps and fording at least three rivers to get to the damaged helicopter. Then he used it to get the semi-submerged helicopter back up onto the beach. Another pilot brought in replacements, including an engine, and they rebuilt the helicopter on the spot before flying it out. As a precaution, they installed floats instead of skids this time.

*While dogs supervise the process, a geophysicist takes a gravimeter reading. As its name suggests, this instrument measured the strength of the gravitational field. On this occasion the survey was funded by, and done for, the US National Space Agency. (Peter Corley-Smith)*

About a month later, they moved from Puntzi Lake right up to Satigi Lake, just south of Aklavik, at the estuary of the Mackenzie River. A week after that, Ian recalls, the helicopter disappeared again: "Mike went off on another of these barometer trips. He said he'd be back by 4 o'clock, but he wasn't, and I wore another trench around my tent. It took us four or five hours to get through to Aklavik [on the radio], where we could get some help to go and look for him."

Eventually a Beaver, belonging to B.C.-Yukon Air Services and flown by company owner Bill Dalzell, was sent from Aklavik into Satigi Lake to start a search. The Beaver's condition shocked Ian Duncan: "He had the most beat-up old Beaver you ever saw in your life. The rudder cables on the floats were so loose, he'd tied knots in them to bring them up to proper tension. You couldn't see the front of the engine for bugs and oil and stuff. You've never seen such a shambles in your life."

Nevertheless they took off in the Beaver to begin the search, and fortunately they quickly found where the helicopter was. Ian Duncan spotted some smoke coming up from a point of land. The first reaction was relief: somebody must be alive. As they circled the point, all they could see were the bottoms of two helicopter floats protruding from the water. When they landed and taxied ashore, they found Mike and his passenger both unhurt, but so badly bitten by mosquitoes that they were in sad shape. This time Mike had fallen victim to glassy water—a condition which makes it impossible to see the surface of the water. He had dug one float in and the machine had flipped on its side. Mike and his pasenger had been able to scramble out before the machine turned over and sank.

Everyone was flown back to camp in the Beaver. Another pilot, Eddy Amman, brought a replacement machine up from Vancouver. Meanwhile, Ian returned to the accident site in the Beaver and after a struggle with "come-alongs" (manually operated ratchet winches) they managed to get the submerged helicopter ashore, where they dismantled it, loaded the pieces into the Beaver and flew them back to camp to start the rebuild. Mike McDonagh was "given a rest" after this second accident and replaced by Bud Tillotson. It was merely a temporary setback for Mike; he went on to a distinguished career as a helicopter pilot.

By 1954, some other operators had begun to use helicopters, and Jock Graham's first job in his new capacity as a technical representative for Pratt and Whitney was with one of them: Hudson Bay Mining. He spent six weeks in a camp some 250 miles north of Teslin Lake in the Yukon. He describes an unnerving maintenance problem which occurred there:

"The pilot, Russ Lennox, kept having the engine almost fail. It looked like fuel starvation. He would land, shut down and then start the engine again and everything would be good. He'd come back to camp and the other engineer and I would just about tear the whole fuel system apart and we couldn't find anything wrong. I was baffled. Then one day we were sitting around with all the sceens [filters] out of the fuel system. One of them was a finger screen—a hollow tube with a fine mesh screen like a thimble on top of it. The mechanic from the Otter we were using picked it up and tried to poke a piece of grass up through the bottom hole. The grass wouldn't go. When I had a good look, I found there was another very fine screen in the hole, where it certainly shouldn't have been. The people who had made the filters for Pratt and Whitney had mis-read the drawings and this extra screen was causing the fuel starvation. So we had to ground every S-55 in North America until the second screen had been punched out. That was quite a worry session."

Anxiety, therefore, was one of the things a helicopter engineer had to live with; boredom was another. The days were long and usually uneventful; the evenings were spent, all too often, in the company of mosquitoes and blackflies, doing routine maintenance.

"You found some things to do," Eric Cowden remembers. "You could usually fish and walk around the shore of the lake, learning something about the vegetation and the animals. But most of the time it was sheer boredom. You had nobody to talk to during the day but

*A "fly camp" wasn't luxurious, as this photo taken by Bob Taylor in 1959 illustrates. Such camps did provide shelter when a minimum of equipment was carried on the helicopter, generally the case on short operations.*

the cook, and he was nearly always a cranky old bastard. I tell you, I've read thousands —and I mean thousands—of pocket books. In fact, I can pick one up even today and probably go through the first paragraph and say, 'Dammit, I've read that one!''

As well as the anxiety and the boredom, there were the living conditions. To go back to Eric and Don Poole's first operation, after their stint at Yehinika Lake and another spell back at Chukachida Lake, they were sent up to Paddy's Lake, some 60 miles south of Atlin, to work with a provincial topographic survey crew. By now they were well into the summer, and living conditions, according to Eric, still had not improved:

"Well, when you were at this camp at Chukachida, you were lucky to get a can of sardines thrown at you. And when we were ferrying from there up to Paddy's Lake, near Atlin —incidentally, by now the old girl was perking along fine; no plug misses or twitches or anything—when we were on the ferry flight, Don suddenly made like he was going to land. And I thought, 'I wonder what that old bugger heard that I didn't hear.'

"Anyway, we landed in a moose patch and I said to Don, 'What the hell did we land here for? 'Well,' he replied, 'you and I have been out a long time; we're going to take ourselves a couple of days off. We're going up to Atlin.' So we poured in our spare gas and when we took off again Don flew much higher than I'd ever seen him fly before, and we went right over Paddy's Lake. Of course, there's a brand new crew down there, all excited, all ready to go to work. They were waving frantically. We pretended we didn't even see them. Old Don was a good 5000 feet and we just chuga-chugged right up into Atlin.

"The first thing we did in Atlin was to go to the cafe and order lunch. And the first thing I ordered was a salad. 'Aren't you going to have a steak?' Don asked. 'Yes, later; but I need to start with this. I think I'm getting scurvy; my gums are all sore.' 'Me, too,' said Don. 'That's why we're here!'

*(Left) Not quite up to Will Tompson's standards but a serviceable shower nevertheless. (Right) The cook is to many the most important man in a bush camp. His skill or lack of it can have considerable influence on the quality of work produced on a job. (Eric Cowden, Peter Corley-Smith)*

"We lived like peasants out there in those days. It was expected of you—part of the job, so you accepted it. Changed days now; nobody'll do it any more."

While it would be an exaggeration to suggest that cases of incipient scurvy were commonplace, they were not unheard of. And many a helicopter crew in the fifties returned to base in the fall looking gaunt, if not emaciated. Ian Duncan talked of two incidents: "That first survey job we did for the Army, we lived on Burns Chuck Wagon Dinners—in the can. That's all we had for the whole season. But that was nothing compared to the second season. That year I was working for an outfit called Fort Reliance Minerals, and I'll never forget that operation. The whole season consisted of dehydrated foods—no bread, no vegetables, no meat. I didn't quite have scurvy, but I was awfully close to it. My gums were all sore and I had lost 36 pounds. At the end of the season I came home and I remember my wife was in tears. I guess I looked some scrawny."

Sometimes these conditions were rationalized by companies with head offices in New York or elsewhere which claimed to believe that Canadians were accustomed to living off the land. Sometimes it was the fault of Canadians themselves, caught up in the ageless syndrome of "You guys just don't know what it was like to live rough." And they would go on to elevate subsistence living to the level of virtue and virility—ignoring the fact that their unfortunate predecessors had usually died young, their health hopelessly impaired by cold, dampness and malnutrition.

It was a passing phase, but a long one for the helicopter crews. They accepted it for a few years, when they were still inexperienced, still a little insecure, trying to "sell" the merits of the helicopter; but as soon as they gained the confidence born of experience, more and more of them began to do what Don and Eric had done. They would jump into the helicopter and fly to the nearest town or settlement for what American servicemen call R and R. With clothes clean and fresh from the laundromat, a few tolerably good meals under their belts, and perhaps a hangover, they would return to camp to face the wrath of the party chief with some equanimity. By the end of the decade, the helicopter business was enjoying an unmistakable boom, so there was little fear of termination. The worst that could happen would be a change of location; a swap with some other crew who were in similar disfavour with their party chief.

The people hiring helicopters for bush exploration soon began to appreciate that if crews became genuinely dissatisfied with living conditions, no amount of attempted coercion could make them productive. A pilot could find a dozen reasons not to fly, ranging from mechanical problems to weather conditions. An engineer could ground the machine for extensive safety checks. It made more sense to improve morale by housing people in weatherproof tents, by feeding them properly, and providing sufficient fixed-wing supply runs to get mail to them at reasonable intervals.

This in turn led to a further problem. Once the customer had decided to provide a reasonable supply of fresh food, it was difficult to find someone who could turn it into a decent meal. Nearly all bush cooks were men who had descended, because of too many losing battles with John Barleycorn, to a state of physical deterioration which left them no option but to become cooks. One day they would find themselves unable to go out and cut line, or drag a chain through the heavy undergrowth to lay out a baseline. They would have to be left in camp to help the cook. From then on, with neither training, talent nor vocation, they would become cooks.

Geologist Will Tompson, party chief for bush operations over the years, recalls that this was his biggest headache. Will believed from his earliest days as a party chief in trying to provide good food and accommodation in a bush camp. He would invariably send in a crew, before the operations began, to build frames of plywood and two-by-fours for the tents. For each two people he provided a 12 by 14 foot canvas tent, with wooden floor (one of those luxuries it is so easy for us to forget), a covering fly and an airtight stove.

Two people, given this sort of accommodation, could live very comfortably in the most extreme temperatures. The fly kept the tent cool when the sun was shining and weatherproof when it was raining. With only a little experience, you could keep an airtight heater smouldering at just the right temperature for indefinite periods. All you needed now to make this resemble something like the comforts of home, was a shower; and this, as Will points out was neither difficult nor unduly expensive: "You don't need to spend a lot of time rigging up showers with 45-gallon drums. You can buy them from any hardware store. The ones I've used are made from steel and come in a square box. Then all you need is a hot water tank, some propane and a few lengths of plastic hose. What the hell, you've got lots of water around, and propane is pretty cheap."

But when it came to cooks, Will had no such easy solutions: "The biggest problem in camp, the most serious problem in exploration, is cooks! The years that Peter Corley-Smith and I worked together we had three bad cooks and one good one. I'd say that's probably about normal. My experience has been that cooks cause more problems than anybody else in the exploration hierarchy."

So this too was one of the disadvantages of the helicopter engineer's lot: he often had to spend his entire day with no other company but the cook. However, like all such generalizations, this one does grave injustice to the one out of four who was a good cook. Theirs was a thankless task, preparing and then cleaning up after three meals a day, seven days a week, for months at a time. If anyone contributed to a successful operation in the bush, it was a good cook.

# CHAPTER 7

# Life in the Bush II

*So I shut down the engine and got out to have a look. Son of a*
*bitch, there was wire wrapped around that helicopter like*
*you never saw.*

BRUCE PAYNE

While life for the helicopter engineer often seems to have been drab and tedious, for the pilot there were some compensations. First, there was the satisfaction of knowing that, practically without exception, everyone in a bush camp would like to have been able to fly the helicopter. They seldom admitted it, of course, but they were all a trifle envious. The pilot was the pivotal figure. It was he who put them all up in those inaccessible mountains or down in the tiny moose pasture in the middle of the tall forest. There was still a touch of magic to it all.

There was also the satisfaction of developing new methods to improve the efficiency of the operation and the value of the helicopter. It was a constant challenge in those first years to work out some method of moving difficult loads. Bruce Payne flew his first season in the bush for Vancouver Island Helicopters in 1956. He speaks now of these events as though they were mere logical extensions of the helicopter's versatility; but at the time they had never been tried, and to try them required some courage:

''I worked for Topo Survey for a couple of years, and then flew for the B.C. Power Commission up in the Homathko River. They were really active in there—a lot of drilling. We had to move the drill rigs—they were the BBS-1 rigs; the engine weighed, oh, about 300-350 pounds and the frame weighed a little more.

''To begin with we had a heck of a time; we used outriggers to move them. We'd put the engine or the frame on the right-hand side, opposite the pilot, and we'd stick a board out the other side about 10 feet long and hang a bag of cement on it . . . to balance the load. It was pretty hairy.

''Then Harvey Jones, or one of the old engineers in VIH, came up with the idea of fixing up part of an old Canso bomb rack and bolting it to the frame under the helicopter so that you could hook on a sling load and jettison it when you needed to. That was a heck of a lot easier than outriggers.

''The drilling jobs were interesting because you were always running into something new. You had to watch yourself, though, or you'd get sucked in. I remember up in the Homathko there, before we started slinging, there was a fellow working for Boyle Brothers, the drilling outfit, a French-Canadian called Paul Roche who'd been up in Kemano before that. We had just finished drilling in this canyon—the landing pad was right in the canyon—and this guy Paul had three tripod poles that he was really fond of. They were 35 feet long, but dry because he'd used them for a couple of months. He wanted me to move them up into Mosely Creek.

''I looked at them and said, 'Heck, there's no way we can move those.' 'Well,' he says, 'we used to move them up in Kemano all the time.' 'How the dickens did you do that?' I asked. 'Show me.' 'Well,' he says, 'we put them on the sides; strapped them right beside the helicopter, on the racks.'

''So we strapped two of these things on, one on either side. They weren't that heavy; they only weighed about 150 pounds apiece. But here we were with these damn things

*The scenery surrounding this fuel cache exemplifies what draws many to bush flying. The helicopter is a Northern Mountain Bell 47-G3B-1. (John King)*

sticking way out in front and way back at the back end. I took off kind of gingerly; but they were okay and I moved them up to Mosely Creek. When I got back, Paul says, 'How did it go?' I says, 'Jesus, it went good; it went good that way.' 'Well,' he says, laughing, 'that's the first time I ever saw *that* done.'

"That sort of thing happened quite often in those days. You had to be pretty careful. The trouble was, you wanted so badly to sell the helicopter you'd try near anything."

Another problem load before slinging came into practice was handling reflector dishes for microwave repeater stations. The dishes always had to be flown to the highest peak. They were about 18 inches deep, 5 feet wide and 12 feet long. Bruce would remove both doors, then climb in and wait while the ground crew tied one on either rack. Once this was done, there was no way for the pilot to get out until the dishes had been untied. It was an uncomfortable feeling. The noise, reflected back at him from the exhaust stacks, was deafening.

No sooner had one load been mastered than another more difficult one would appear. Bruce recalls that the microwave dishes grew larger: "One reflector in particular, I remember. I had to fly it up the mountain from Little Prairie, which is Chetwynd now. It was a great big one; I think it was 22 feet long, but it was the same depth and width. I couldn't put this one on the side because it was too heavy, so I tied it underneath the helicopter. I started off down this strip—there was a little old grass strip there—and when I got up to about 20 miles an hour, the cyclic [control column] was well back in my stomach, yet the nose kept on going down. The wind was hitting the front of the dish and driving the nose down. Well, I had just enough control left to slow down again and get the nose up. Then I hovered up the side of that mountain at 15 miles an hour. It was a slow climb."

For Bruce, the next innovations came when helicopters began to be used for hydro power line construction. Once the survey had been completed and the tower sites located, landing pads were built at each site. Ground crews would then be flown in to construct the forms for the concrete tower footings. Then the concrete, already mixed at a central point, would be flown in. Bruce describes the method:

"Most of the buckets at that time were 45-gallon drums. We'd just put a ring on the bottom of them. Then you'd lay the drum onto the edge of the form, a guy on the ground would transfer your lanyard clip onto this ring and you'd lift up and dump it for them. Later on we got the self-dumping buckets. You'd just hover over the form, a guy on the ground would pull a lever and it would dump itself."

Once the footings were poured, the helicopter would start to sling in the steel for the tower. Sometimes, with the smaller helicopters, they would actually hang the tower steel, length by length, while the ground crew bolted them into place. Later, with the advent of the larger helicopters, the Sikorsky S-58s and the Bell 204Bs, whole sections of the tower would be dropped into place.

The next stage would be the installation of the cables. Once again the helicopter could speed things up enormously. The process began with the stringing of what is called a sock line—a thin steel cable, perhaps a quarter of an inch in diameter, which would later be used to pull the actual power cables into position.

This sock line would be on a large drum, mounted on the back of a flat-bed truck. The drum had a brake on it, operated manually, to allow the line to be paid out at a steady ten-

*The installation of microwave dishes on towers was exacting work, requiring capable people both in the helicopter and on the tower. Cockpit visibility from the S-55 was less than ideal. (Okanagan Helicopters Collection)*

*In the mid-1950s this British-built Bristol Sycamore came to Canada on a promotion tour. Shown here in the Fraser Valley, the helicopter, which was successful elsewhere, failed to find customers in North America. It was too light to fit in the medium-lift category, and too difficult to maintain in the bush as a light general-purpose type. (Alf Stringer)*

sion. A metal ball weighing 150 to 200 pounds would be slung below the helicopter. Bruce describes the procedure: "The ball hung about 20 feet below the helicopter and they'd hook the line on to that. Then I'd just move out and pull it off the ground. I've pulled out as much as 42,000 feet with a Bell 47. What's that? About seven miles, I guess. It would take up to five minutes to get it moving."

On at least one occasion, it took longer than that. After pulling maximum climb power for some 10 minutes, Bruce finally gave up, dropped the ball and flew the mile or so back to the drum truck to find out what was wrong. When he got there, he found the operator sound asleep, with the brake firmly set.

When he had got the sock line moving, the pilot would pass each tower and then back up to give the ground crew enough slack to run the line through a "traveller" or pulley, which would then be pulled up and secured to the cross-arms on top of the tower. Once the length for that particular section had been run out, another truck with a winch would hook on to the sock line and pull the actual power cable, which was attached to the tail end of it, through the travellers.

"It wasn't a bad job," according to Bruce, "but some of the guys couldn't take it. They could pull sock line on the flat ground, or the not-so-hilly stuff—but when they got over one of those big valleys, with a thousand feet of nothing underneath them, and they're sitting there at, oh, maybe three or four miles an hour for 20 maybe 30 minutes, pulling it across, then they'd get vertigo pretty bad and have a real problem."

Most of the hydro construction was done by private companies under contract to B.C. Hydro. The final task, after construction was completed, was for the helicopter pilot to take out the Hydro inspectors. As a rule he would land them on the pad near the base of each tower and they would climb the tower to make sure that all the bolts were in place and secure and that the insulators and cables were correctly installed. However, if the weather was calm and the pilot feeling intrepid, he could balance on the cross-arms on the top of the tower, drop his passengers and then pick them up on the pad below when they had completed their inspection. It was a popular pilot who was willing to do this.

These developments were stimulating and satisfying when they worked. When they did not, the result could be an accident. Those involved had to learn to be philosophical about accidents; they were part of the learning process, and few pilots went very long without one. The tail rotor, hanging out of sight some 20 feet behind the pilot's back was an Achilles Heel. It was so easy, when landing in a bush clearing, to poke it into the stump of a rotted tree or a clump of willow. In the early days, all loads had to be carried on the external racks. It was often hard to estimate how much weight was on board, and once one was commit-

*A Hiller 1100 about to hook up to the sockline on a hydro construction project. (Fairchild-Hiller)*

*A pilot would occasionally be able to ake his family along. Bell 47-G3B-1, CF-VIH, was the pride of the Vancouver Island Helicopters fleet when this photo was taken in the 1960s. (Peter Corley-Smith)*

ted to take off all that was needed to start trouble was a plug choking up—something not uncommon with the Franklin engine.

Fortunately the advent of the cargo hook relieved this problem. You could punch off the load if needed. Apart from the machine itself, perhaps the biggest hazard was posed by wires which stretched, usually unmarked, across rivers and valleys. Bruce Payne describes an encounter with wires early in his career:

"I had been on fisheries patrols, counting fish, with a biologist called Mac Chapman. I'd been doing this job on and off for a couple of years, up and down the river—it was in connection with the dam work on the Fraser and its tributaries.

"The wires we hit were thick ones, almost as thick as your finger. They crossed the Fraser just below Tejeune. I still can't figure how I didn't see them. We'd been up and down this stretch of river two years before—in fact, we'd been up and down it earlier the same day, and neither of us saw those wires.

"I guess I just got low enough that run. I ran right into them. I saw them just about the time we flew into them. They hit the bubble about eye-level. They didn't break the bubble; they went up over it and into the mast. Then the blades caught them and they made an awful racket. That slowed the blades down and we just dropped right into the river bed; we landed in the water. It was only three or four inches deep, but it was muddy and we were settling into this stuff.

"So I shut down the engine and got out to have a look. Son of a bitch, there was wire wrapped round that helicopter like you never saw. You know the scissors levers [two control arms running up on either side of the mast to alter the pitch of the rotor blades], they were just strapped right into the mast, tight."

The option to give up and wade ashore was not available: they were on a mud bank in the middle of the river, with deep water on either side. So Bruce and his passenger set about unravelling the wire. It took them more than half-an-hour. The wooden rotor blades were damaged, but Bruce replaced the shards of wood which had come off the leading edges and taped them into place with the black friction tape pilots always carried in a helicopter. Next he climbed up and pulled out the scissors levers until they were more or less straight and parallel with the mast. By this time the machine had sunk almost a foot into the mud.

"So we got back in," Bruce continues, "and I fired up. It was pretty rough—things were out of balance—but I managed to move her up onto a little bench on the bank of the river, where I shut down again so that I could take a really good look at the blades. I thought, gee, maybe I can balance those things out. There was no radio, and nowhere we could've walked to from there, so I started wrapping tape on those blades. I started up and shut down several times, and in the end I got it so it wasn't too bad. Then we had a real good look, the two of us, and couldn't see any . . . you know, there were quite a few nicks and creases from that flaming wire. So in the end we climbed in and flew back to Prince George . . . about an hour-and-a-half. It was rough as hell, but the tape held okay and we made it."

Helicopters even from their earliest days were generally reliable, but there were occasional bad "runs" when mechanical problems caused many a fast pulse. There was a period with the Bells in the middle fifties when some flaw in the manufacturing process caused many fan-belt failures. The Franklin engines were cooled by a large fan, belt-driven from the engine. The fan sat no more than six or eight inches behind the pilot's back, separated only by what was rather euphemistically called a firewall—a thin and remarkably resonant sheet of metal. When a fan belt let go, it invariably flailed into the firewall with a report like a rifle shot—a noise that would jerk even the coolest pilot hard up against his seat belt. He had to find a landing within two or three minutes or the engine would overheat and seize up. Over densely forested country, this could be a long and sometimes breathless time.

Another of these "runs" occurred with the advent of the Hiller 12E in the late fifties. This was Bell's competition in the light helicopter category; it was a very responsive machine, giving the impression of increased power and load capacity. But those who used it ran into teething troubles. Bruce describes the problems he had in the early sixties: "I was working on a seismic survey for an outfit called General Geophysical—a Texas company on contract to Shell Oil. We were working along the Redstone Dehadinni River, just to the west of the Mackenzie, between Wrigley and Norman Wells. That was a bad, bad one, that job."

When asked what was so bad about it, Bruce hesitated. "I don't think people will believe it now if you tell what conditions were like in those days." Apparently this had been one of the first big seismic surveys by helicopter. Lines had to be cut and surveyed, and drills and compressors had to be carried, as well as the dynamite for the seismic shots. The bidding for the contract had been very competitive, and General Geophysical had to pare expenses to the bone in order to make a profit. Some 75 to 80 men were employed, four to a pup tent. Packs and suitcases had to be stored outside, under a ground sheet. They were working two shifts, and each man had to share his sleeping bag with his opposite number on the other shift—four of them could not have fitted into the tent at once. The helicopter crews considered themselves lucky. At least they had their own sleeping bags.

But the more serious problem was food. The company had decided they could not afford to fly in fresh food, so the food all had to be trucked up the Mackenzie Highway to Hay River, then transferred to barges to be towed up and dropped on the river bank some 30 miles from their main camp. Unfortunately communications were so poor they seldom heard that a load of food had been dropped until a week or 10 days later. By the time they did hear, the bears had usually got to it first—and most of it had gone bad. ''The cooks used to ask you, 'Do you want one egg this week, or two next week?' It was that sort of deal.''

''Anyway,'' Bruce went on, ''we had three engine failures in 19 days. They were all on Hillers. I was flying along one night and picked up a couple of guys about two o'clock in the morning—it was light almost 24 hours a day. Every half-mile there was an opening in the trees. I was going right down this cut line, heading for camp with these guys—they'd had some problems—and the first thing I saw was some oil splattering on the bubble above me. Then there was a terrific noise and a rod let go; it came right out the side of the crankcase, and that was it; we were going down.

''Right about then there was this opening, and I just flared the helicopter and we went down into it and landed. A second either way and it wouldn't have worked. It was just there. I had to wait until next morning, though, before anyone came and found me.

''The next one I had was at night again, but this time there was a fixed-wing following me. We'd moved a crew and we were going back into camp; it was a [Cessna] 185 and he saw me go down, so they knew where I was. I had a passenger with me and a drill compressor slung on the hook underneath when the engine started running rough. It got rougher and rougher and then it just went *brrrmmmhh*—that was it. But this time I was over muskeg. I punched off the compressor and landed without bending anything. The engineer came out, put new mags on and we flew her out.''

The next incident, unfortunately for Bruce, was more serious, and it occurred only a few days later: ''I'd moved a crew of Indians—line cutters—and had lunch with them. After lunch the foreman and I got into the machine to go back to camp. We used to run through the old preamble with those Hillers. Start the engine and then let it run for a few minutes to warm everything up. We were in an old burn on top of a knob. They'd just cut out a little landing for me; they were going to clear out a bigger area later.

''So I got ready to take off, opened the throttle up to rpm and lifted off. There were dead trees, about 50 or 60 feet tall all around, and I'd just got over them when the engine quit, just like that. Down we went into the trees—there was wood flying all over the place. Without power, I lost tail-rotor control and the machine turned sideways to the slope. We hit the ground so hard that the legs on the skids were snapped right off and we flipped on our side and caught fire.

''Up to then it hadn't been too bad. Neither of us was hurt, but the fellow with me was above me now. There were flames shooting up behind us pretty high, and he got scared. He sure messed up my face getting out of there; his old feet started to flail. Anyways, we got out all right, and I put the fire out with the extinguisher.

''I should have let it burn. We had a hell of a time getting it out of there. We took it out to the river, put it on a barge and it went up to Norman Wells. Then they found they couldn't get it into a DC-6. So it went back on the barge and all the way down to Hay River to be trucked down to Vancouver. They never got it home until wintertime. Heck, I should've let it burn.''

To a pilot, accidents were a source of constant concern. Even though he might be blameless, the company's insurance premiums would rise. The Department of Transport, nomi-

*Pacific Helicopters Hiller 12-E at Banner Ranger Station, June 1960. (British Columbia Ministry of Forests)*

nally the overseer of flight safety in the bush, in reality played little part in the enforcement of regulations. It was the insurance companies which kept watch. In the eyes of the actuaries, the pilot could never win. If he had a number of accidents, he became a high risk. If he had none, the argument was that all helicopter pilots had accidents; he was due for one and was a high risk!

On the whole, life for helicopter crews in the bush was a mixture of much discomfort and occasional satisfaction; of considerable boredom punctuated by flurries of excitement. The long spells of isolation and in some cases deprivation were usually followed by parties which, in their eyes, became memorable. Ian Duncan describes the celebrations at the end of one season:

"We all ended up in Aklavik. Dayton Reid and his pilot Snuffy Foster, Bud Tillotson and myself—the two crews had both landed there at the same time; we were both ready to ferry out at the end of the season. So you have to have a party. We went down to the liquor store and got all the booze we could and had a horrendous flipping party, just marvellous. I can remember going *bblllmmmmmmmbb* in front of the old hotel. Must've been something I ate.

"Anyway, we all went to this North Star hotel. It was a tiny little place, but they had a partition you could fold aside to make one room if you wanted to have a dance. There was one on that night, run by the Eskimo girls. So of course we all had to go to the dance and we were somewhat into our cups when we arrived. There was a young Mountie standing at the door, being very officious. We were dancing around and I paused when I got near this fellow—I was feeling very happy, fatuously happy, I suppose—and I said, 'Look, Constable,' I said, 'if there's going to be any shooting, let's have it outside—outside the building.' He wasn't amused. In fact, he was incensed, and I moved on smartly.

"I had seen Bud dancing with a little Eskimo girl and he was having a great time. I saw him pass by and he said something to the Mountie, too. Next time I looked round, Bud was gone. The girl he had been dancing with was standing alone. I went up to her. 'Where's my friend?' I asked.

"She said, 'The policeman just took him to jail there. I seen him put him in the car and took him away there and put him in jail.'

"'Well, I'm going to get him out,' I told her. 'You much better not,' she replied. 'They put you in jail there too.'

"I had just enough sense left to realize she was right. But the next morning Snuffy Foster went down to bail Bud out. The magistrate was the CO of the Navy Communications Centre at Aklavik. Snuffy got nowhere with him. 'Look, buddy,' he said, 'there are two Eskimo boys involved in this, too. They've been charged and you don't get any different treatment than they do.'

"So Snuffy came back to tell us the bad news and we all went down to court, which was the church. We all sat in the back pew, and there's the constable sitting there and the magistrate.

"The two Eskimos were tried first. They both pleaded guilty. They were fined 10 dollars, and four dollars court costs. The magistrate asked them if they could pay. They both asked for a couple of days, and the magistrate agreed.

"Then came Bud's turn. Bud had a hearing problem. When he didn't hear what was said, and he was a bit rattled, he used to say 'Ehhh?' in a loud voice. And sure enough, when he gets on the stand and the judge asks him, 'Do you plead guilty or not guilty?' Bud says, 'Ehhh?' and we started to break up in the back pew. 'Order in Court!' He asks him again and Bud hears him this time and pleads guilty.

"The magistrate says, 'Ten dollars and four dollars costs. Do you have that, Mr. Tillotson?'

"Bud takes out his wallet and gazes into it with a look of dismay. You don't carry much cash in the bush, and he'd spent all his on booze the night before. He looked so funny, gazing sadly into his empty wallet. This time we really broke up; we were just about falling out of the pew, and I think the magistrate was having a little trouble keeping his face straight.

"Anyway, in the end we managed to come up with 14 dollars between us and they let Bud go."

Asked what Bud had said to the Mountie to get himself arrested, Ian chuckled. "He just asked him if he could have the next dance, and this little turkey took umbrage and ran him in for drunk and disorderly. Hell, we were all drunk and disorderly. Who wouldn't be after a long season in the bush?"

The celebrations were uncomplicated and the humour unsophisticated. The incidents remembered usually depended on the personalities involved. In this case the victim, Bud Tillotson, was such an amiable and unaggressive person that it made people who knew him burst out laughing to hear that he had been arrested for disorderly conduct. For many years Bud ran the mountain training course for Okanagan Helicopters from Penticton. He is always spoken of with respect and affection.

Another pilot who is spoken of in the same way is Fred Eilertson. Wherever he happened to be, flying in the bush or attending to business in the city, Fred was always dressed in a tweed jacket and a floppy tweed hat. Not surprisingly, he became known as Tweedy and so firmly did this nickname become attached to him that some people have trouble remembering his actual name. But they never have trouble remembering the man.

Tweedy had a slight hesitation in his speech and this, combined with his unconventional bush clothes, led many an unwary bush worker to think he was a little slow-witted. Tweedy could handle this sort of thing. Given an aggressive party chief who would jump into the helicopter and order the pilot to take him somewhere, Tweedy would look around at the instruments and switches vaguely, then open the door, lean out and say to the engineer in a loud voice, "H-H-How do you s-start this thing?"

Ian Duncan recalls an incident early on in their careers, when he and Tweedy went to Laidlaw to move a crew into the Reco Copper Mine. They had to move nine men into the mine at the 6300-foot level, in one of the early 47-D1s. Tweedy was taking them in one at a time, and after a while Ian noticed that one individual kept going to the end of the line. It

*A.Y. Jackson, one of the celebrated Group of Seven painters, travelled in this Bell 47 on one of his trips north in the early 1960s. (Peter Corley-Smith)*

was obvious he was nervous. He didn't want to fly in the helicopter. So when his time came and he had to climb into the passenger seat, Ian opened the door on Tweedy's side and advised him that he had a very nervous passenger.

"Thanks for telling me. I appreciate it."

When Tweedy returned, 20 minutes later, Ian asked, "How did it go?" "Well, p-p-pretty interesting," he replied. Apparently the passenger had begun by jamming himself into the seat, his feet pressed hard against the stubs into which rudder pedals were inserted when dual controls were needed for instruction.

"If you d-don't take you f-f-feet off those I can't s-steer and we'll c-crash," Tweedy advised him. The passenger moved his feet and after a few minutes began to relax a little and study the instrument panel. He asked about one instrument and Tweedy told him it was the altimeter. He asked about another and Tweedy explained that it was the tachometer. Finally, the passenger's eye fell on the fuel gauge. The fuel gauges in the early models were notoriously unreliable; the needle invariably hovered around the empty mark, and pilots had long since taken to using a dip stick to measure the fuel in their tank. However, when Tweedy told him what the guage was for, his passenger's eyes widened. "But it's on the E," he protested. "Don't that mean empty?"

"Yeah," Tweedy agreed, "but with a b-b-bit of luck, I think we'll make it."

When Tweedy landed up on the mine site and his passenger was getting out, he said to him, "I'll be back in a couple of weeks to p-p-pick you up."

"No you won't," replied the passenger. "I'm going to walk down!"

*Returning from the Liard-Matu Rivers area where they had been doing seismic testing for Shell Oil, this Okanagan crew of (left to right) Bill Legge, Ian Duncan, Rod Fraser and Fred "Tweedy" Eilertson stopped at Ashcroft. Legge and Eilertson were pilots, and Duncan and Fraser engineers. The Sikorsky S-55 CF-GHV was purchased from Alcan by Okanagan after the Kemano project. (Ian Duncan)*

# CHAPTER 8

# Helicopters in Forestry

*Sometimes a pilot would spot a chokerman's lunch sitting on
a stump and would very precisely drop the 60-pound hook on
it with inevitable results.*

WALTER PALUBISKI

Possibly the most eloquent demonstration of the helicopter's versatility is in forestry, where tasks include basic transportation, pest control, logging and fire suppression.

One of the earliest contracts awarded to the newly-organized Okanagan Air Services in July 1948 was to spray forests in the Windermere Valley in the Kootenays to counter an infestation of the spruce budworm. While the helicopter had proven less than successful for spraying small orchards in the Okanagan, it proved ideal in this instance, the downwash from the rotor blades spreading the insecticide. In the mid-1950s helicopters were used to spray log booms with insecticide. The submerged portions of the logs were not in danger but the upper portions, exposed to destructive insects, were suffering severe damage. A helicopter was by far the most effective means of countering this threat because it was able to cover large surface areas quickly.

In November 1951 the Forestry Division of MacMillan Bloedel undertook the first aerial re-seeding of logged-off areas in British Columbia. Two sites were chosen for the experiment: Alberni Pacific Camp One and the Chemainus Division Copper Canyon logging operations. The work began using a Hiller 360 owned and flown by Dean Johnson of McMinnville, Oregon. Initially Johnson laid rodent bait on 1760 acres of logged off land at Camp One. If the poisoned bait had not been laid, forest mice would have quickly disposed of tree seeds. The helicopter, flying at 60 mph, could cover 24 acres a minute laying bait in 200-foot-wide swaths. A week after dropping the bait, the helicopter repeated the process over the same territory, this time sowing Douglas fir and hemlock seeds. The process of laying bait was subsequently repeated over 2500 acres in the Copper Canyon area. The helicopter laid the bait and seed from two side-mounted hoppers, the devices being set to spread 25,000 seeds per acre. The helicopter allowed reforestation to be carried out more quickly than otherwise possible. Easily accessible timber resources could be renewed.

A considerable proportion of British Columbia's high value first-growth timber resources —most estimates are in the vicinity of 15 per cent of the total—have until recently been inaccessible to loggers due to rough terrain and constant, steep sidehills. Conventional methods are inadequate in such circumstances, being uneconomical and often physically impossible. One proposed solution to the problem was to use captive balloons to bring logs out—the ultimate high-lead yarding. A number of experiments were carried out by the Skegs Forsknings Institutein in Sweden in 1956-57 and in British Columbia in 1963, 1968 and 1971 at Vancouver, Sproat Lake and Hope respectively. While the system worked to a degree, a major disadvantage with balloons, and one that virtually negates their feasibility in many areas of the province, became apparent. They could not be used when winds climbed to 25 mph or above. The helicopter, which is not as subject to winds, appeared to offer much better potential.

By the late 1950s the size of helicopters was increasing and they were establishing themselves in the "skyhook" role. Indications were that they could be the means of harvesting inaccessible stands of timber. It was likely too that helicopters would be safer in the woods during fire season since the chokers on the logs would not be dragged along the ground sending sparks into the dry underbush as they hit rocks. In addition, there would likely be less environmental impact since it would be unnecessary to construct logging roads or rail lines. Theoretically the advantages and capabilities were there, but it would require considerable experimentation with aircraft and equipment before operations could be undertaken.

The first significant experiment with heli-logging in British Columbia was carried out in 1971. OK Lifts Limited, a subsidiary of Okanagan Helicopters, logged experimentally on the Richmond Plywood quota of timber on Redonda Island, 27 miles east of Campbell River. Between June 3 and June 24, 1971, Grant Soutar of Okanagan flew an S-58T often carrying up to three logs, or approximately 750 board feet, at a time. This load used the helicopter's 5000-pound payload to its maximum. Logs were hauled two miles from the sidehill on East Redonda to the drop zone in Pendrell Sound. There were three objectives in this experiment: to test the aircraft as a logging vehicle; to develop and try methods; and to see if the combination was economical. With an average of 5-1/2 flying hours a day, 1400 logs were hauled out during the three-week experiment. The only major problem was the hook to which the cable used to lift the logs was attached. For both safety and speed, a quick re-

*Dean Johnson of Portland, Oregon, used this early Hiller, a model 360, in British Columbia's first attempt at aerial reseeding of a forest. (*Harmac News*)*

*Forests can be devastated by insects. In June 1962 this helicopter was pressed into service spraying pesticides, in this case phytoactin, to combat an outbreak of white pan blister rust. (British Columbia Ministry of Forests)*

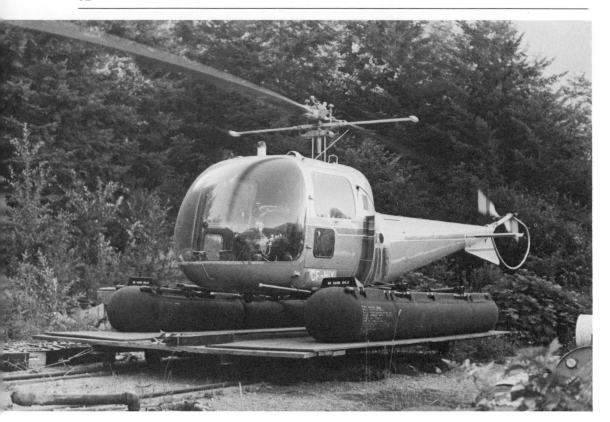

*Many logging companies have their own helicopters. Williams Logging of Spuzzum in the Fraser Canyon used this Bell 47-J2 in the mid-1970s. (R.D. Turner)*

lease mechanism was used. This had considerable spring-back tension and it was found that after the load was released, bolts in the mechanism were often sheared off and sometimes the hook itself was broken. This problem was solved by Okanagan, and another hurdle towards making heli-logging feasible was overcome.

In March 1974 Okanagan was once again involved in heli-logging on Vancouver Island, this time in the Port Alberni region. Along with MacMillan Bloedel and the Tahsis Company, Okanagan was hoping to determine the economics of heli-logging by carrying out tests over a period of three to five weeks. Dave Turner, MacMillan Bloedel vice-president in charge of logging, stated that two concepts were being tested. The first was the comparative merits of hauling logs from the logging site to water dumps or hauling to dry sort areas. Environmentalists were increasingly concerned about saltwater dumping since a large amount of debris inevitably remained in the water. The second was to try harvesting previously fallen logs from areas where second growth had taken over. The feasibility seemed to depend on the height of the second-growth trees—ground crew could be obscured. When this was tried again some years later in the Prince Rupert region, it once again proved difficult for the helicopter crew to spot the chokerman below the canopy of second-growth trees, so various methods of locating the man on the ground were considered, such as using a powerful strobe light hand-held by the chokerman, using a balloon which would ascend above the canopy and serve as a marker, or simply having the chokerman direct the helicopter by radio. The last proved to be the only method that worked according to Okanagan heli-logging manager Walter Palubiski.

*This ex-United States Navy Sikorsky SH-3, owned by Boise-Cascade and leased by Okanagan, was used in heli-logging experiments in British Columbia in the late 1970s. It has a hook capacity of approximately 10,000 pounds. (British Columbia Ministry of Forests)*

In sharp contrast to the excellent relations today, difficulties with labour complicated the experiment. Ken Blackwood, who oversaw the operation for Okanagan, recalled: "The Union more or less sabotaged the experiments—apparently didn't want to see the new technology come in. Initially everyone was enthusiastic since they were all eager to get their first helicopter ride but they still demanded three hours travel time; then the fallers apparently felt that they could help out the 'troops' by not allowing us to haul according to plan. The scale cuts for bucking they cut too light and too short or too long. Instead of falling timber in a parallel fashion the way they were requested, they started building big jackpots [piles], so it affected our production in such a way that it was not cost effective or economical."

The union failed to recognize that heli-logging was complementary to conventional methods, not in competition with them. No union jobs would be affected for different timber stands were involved. Moreover, the expense of heli-logging precluded its use where conventional methods worked.

The experiments were successful from Okanagan's standpoint since they proved that heli-logging was technically practical, but the logging companies were still not entirely convinced. They thought, as had nearly all customers when using helicopters for the first time, that the costs were too high to be acceptable. Experiments were again undertaken, this time on Cortes Island in the summer of 1977 with an Okanagan Bell 214. Despite the fact that the 214 was too small to be economical in logging service and the job was very hard on the aircraft as well, this experiment was successful. Three companies, T.M.

Thomson Associates, Trace-Mahood and Okanagan, had formed Heli Aero Logging Limited for this operation and by its end had logged 4500 cunits.

Okanagan's Heavy Lift Division, despite the fact Okanagan was an aviation, not a logging company, decided that the best means of harvesting otherwise inaccessible timber would be to have their own ground crews. Walter Palubiski recalls that workers came from a somewhat surprising source:

"Initially a high percentage of our ground crew came from Victoria. I guess word spread quickly among university students that we were looking for help. Later, people also came from communities near our operations such as Campbell River. Few, if any, of the university applicants had had any logging experience and so we had to train them ourselves. Despite their inexperience they proved to be very willing, hard workers who were enthusiastic about working with helicopters—there was a form of romanticism attached to it. It wasn't unusual for these people to come in at the end of a shift and enquire about the day's quota. Relations between ground and air crews were extremely good, a necessity in heli-logging.

"As in any situation where morale is very high, there were practical jokes—it was necessary for a man on the ground to take out rain gear and food since he was going to be out for up to twelve hours at a stretch. Sometimes a pilot would spot a chokerman's lunch sitting on a stump and would very precisely drop the 60-pound hook on it with inevitable results. The air waves would usually be filled with comments that didn't bear repeating. We had to put a stop to that."

The S-61 along with the S-64 and the Vertol 107 have proven to be the most suitable helicopters for logging. The machines used by Okanagan, all of which are S-61Ls, come from two sources: on lease and then purchase from Boise-Cascade, and by purchase from New York Airways. The former were configured as logging helicopters when acquired, the others were converted from airliners. The ex-New York Airways aircraft had their interiors stripped down to the exposed airframe to reduce weight. Pressed into service on arrival in B.C., vestiges of their former liveries in some cases persisted into 1981 before repainting into Okanagan colours. Those S-61s used in logging exclusively are not equipped for instrument flying as are others used by Okanagan for resupplying drill rigs and other transportation duties. Moreover a logging S-61 on the job carries only one hour's fuel, 150 gallons, because weight is a critical factor. The more the aircraft weighs, the less load it can sling.

It normally takes two years in heli-logging for an S-61 captain to become thoroughly proficient at placing a hook quickly and precisely over the chokerman, who has attached a 26-foot cable to the log, and hoist it out as efficiently as possible. The S-61 carries a two-man crew, both qualified command pilots on type. The pilot, while at the controls, concerns himself exclusively with flying the aircraft and with the load. The other pilot monitors the instruments and records the weight of the load from a digital readout situated on the right-hand side of the instrument panel. This enables the crew to ensure that the load is within acceptable limits, and to keep track of the amount being hauled.

The load itself is attached to the helicopter by means of three hooks: one on the belly of the machine, a second attached to a shock absorber, and a third at the bottom end of a 140-foot line. The choker or chokers, depending on the load, are attached to the third hook. If the load is too heavy, or if it is caught in the ground cover, it is possible to punch it off at any of the three connecting points. The pilot can do this simply by pressing a button on the cyclic control column. The whole operation of picking up a load is controlled by the loadmaster who is in communication with the pilot by radio. Up to two months before the heli-loggers move into an area, a crew of fallers go out to cut trees, falling them as much as possible in parallel to permit more efficient hoisting by the helicopters.

The Sikorsky S-64 was designed specifically as a flying crane, initially with piston engines, later with turbines. It could be used for passenger or freight loads by attaching a "van." (Below) Silver Grizzly Timber Company operated the Skycrane from this floating base at Khutzeywateen Inlet. (Both, British Columbia Ministry of Forests)

*(Left) Helicopters, like this Bell 206 shown at Mica Creek, are used to drop water on fires. Monsoon buckets are available in varying sizes and the amount of water each contains can be regulated by removing plugs. (Right) Rapattack helicopters are specially equipped with connecting points for the lines, and they carry a crewman who acts as a spotter. The bag suspended above the firefighter contains his equipment. (Both, British Columbia Ministry of Forests)*

The logs can be repositioned by the helicopters, but if this is necessary, time may be lost. Limbs are removed from trees at this time as well, except for those situated on the inaccessible side of the log. Loadmasters are trained to estimate weights of logs. A formula that has proven to be very accurate was worked out by Okanagan in 1978. This still requires a loadmaster to be proficient, since log weights can vary according to location —the amount of moisture absorbed by the log can throw the formula off.

Meanwhile other companies moved into the province, some initially inexperienced like Okanagan. Bow Helicopters of Calgary was among the earliest operators to experiment with logging when it moved into the Pitt Lake region in June 1972, working under contract to Higher Profit Research and Development of Vancouver. Experiments apparently proved successful since the latter company was soon talking about using S-61s in the Jervis Inlet area. This scheme did go ahead, but with another company.

Five years after the Pitt Lake experiment, an experienced American operator began operations in British Columbia, initially employing few Canadians but increasing the numbers as experience was gained. This firm, Columbia Helicopters Limited, of Portland, Oregon, used the Kawasaki KV-107/II, a Japanese-built version of the Boeing Vertol 107/II. This was a medium-lift type very much like the CH-113A helicopters used by the Canadian Forces. Columbia worked both Drury and Seymour Inlets, the former on the quota of a wholly-owned subsidiary, Jewell Timber, and the latter under contract to MacDonald Cedar Products Limited, a firm that had earlier supported the idea of helicopter logging. The operation was successful, profits varying with the "show" and location. The MacDonald Cedar Products operation in 1978 involved an area of 150 acres from which it was hoped that close to 5.5 million board feet could be removed.

Another American firm which has operated in British Columbia is Erickson Air-Cranes, which works the Silver Grizzly timber quota in the Prince Rupert region. This operation differs little from others except for the logging aircraft—an enormous Sikorsky S-64 Sky-crane, a heavy-lift machine carrying loads of up to 20,000 pounds, twice that carried by the S-61 or KV-107. Two of these machines have been in use with Silver Grizzly since 1977, but one crashed in 1981. While the Okanagan, Columbia, and Silver Grizzly operations are spectacular, they have not been the only helicopter logging companies in British Columbia. Skyhook of Courtenay logged on Vancouver Island using a Hiller 12E, and Transwest Helicopters of Pitt Meadows worked in the Pitt Lake area for several years using a Bell 204 and later a 214 which subsequently crashed at Bella Coola while fighting a forest fire. The 12E and 204 are classed as utility helicopters and are typical of others used in various aspects of logging such as general transportation and, in heli-logging, moving the ground crews and retrieving the chokers.

Helicopters have proven extremely valuable in all aspects of forest fire suppression: setting out lookout towers, transporting fire fighters and their equipment, and water-bombing. From its earliest use in forestry, the helicopter has carried firefighters directly to a blaze. Covering the same ground on foot is time-consuming and difficult when speed is so vital. The sooner a fire is caught the better.

While basic transportation is vital in fire suppression, and was initially the most important task for helicopters, it was not long before they were also used for observation. Fire bosses (those in charge of fighting the fire) used them to watch progress of the fire and plan strategy accordingly. They could decide in advance where to place crews and equipment and where to create fire breaks. If necessary, the helicopter could be used to quickly remove a threatened crew from the path of a fire that had changed direction. Prompt medevac was now possible in the event of accident, something that boosted crew morale.

The first use of a tanker helicopter in British Columbia took place in 1958 when

Okanagan converted an S-58. The cabin was fitted with a 225-gallon tank and appropriate plumbing, and discharge ''gates'' were cut in the belly of the aircraft. The S-58 was used to extinguish a fire near the headwaters of the Ashlu and Squamish Rivers. Alf Stringer when asked about the conversion commented that it created a significant problem. With its conversion, the S-58 ceased to be a general purpose machine and became exclusively a tanker. This was impractical.

Jim Grady, Nelson base manager for Okanagan Helicopters, is generally credited, in British Columbia at least, with the invention in the early 1960s of the ''monsoon bucket.'' In its earliest form, it was simple: a 45-gallon drum filled with water, with a basketball plugging a hole in the bottom. Hovering over a fire with the bucket suspended on a sling, Grady would pull on a line attached to the ball. The ball would be pulled up against the weight of water above it, uncorking the drum—Grady must have had a strong right arm. The water cascaded out onto the fire, extinguishing or least retarding it. The bucket was adopted by Okanagan and before long others were using similar rigs. More recent versions bear little resemblance to the original; they are of lightweight plastic which can be rolled up and stored, and have various capacities; in some the capacity can be altered by the removal of plugs in the sides of the bucket. An electrically-actuated solenoid operates the trap-door mechanism, replacing the crude ball and line that Grady used.

The monsoon bucket has several advantages over the extensive S-58 conversion. Any general utility helicopter can use one since all that is required is a belly hook and an electrical connection. The bucket can be readily attached or detached. It can be filled by simply hovering over water, or other fire retardant. Not having to land decreases turn-around time between loads. The bucket, when not in use for fire fighting, can be used to transport supplies and equipment without the helicopter landing. The primary use of a monsoon bucket is in extinguishing small flareups or ''hotspots'' after the main fire has been extinguished. They are unsuitable for use on large fires as they have limited impact.

A disadvantage of the monsoon bucket is that it releases water slowly as compared to a fixed-wing tankers like the Canso or A-26. This increases the time the helicopter must remain over a blaze, which in turn may result in the fire being fanned by downwash and embers blown about to start other fires.

Another way of converting the helicopter into a tanker without compromising its other functions is used by Frontier Helicopters. A detachable belly tank of much greater capacity than the monsoon buckets is used. It has the additional advantage of having bomb-bay doors to regulate the quantity and pattern of the drop. A major disadvantage is that turnaround time is increased as the tank must be refilled on the ground.

Rappelling, a technique used by the Canadian Forces and others to land infantry from a hovering helicopter, has been adopted in forest fire suppression. Rappellers slide down to the ground on ropes, from above tree-top level if necessary. First used operationally in the summer of 1977, ''rapattack,'' as it has been termed in British Columbia, has proven effective in putting crews in to fight fires set by lightning strikes. Frequently there are no suitable landing spots near a fire and rappelling is the only means of getting a crew in to deal with a blaze that can spread with frightening speed. Rapattack headquarters, which coordinates operations over the province, is situated in the Kamloops Forest region in Salmon Arm, the training base for the program.

Only Frontier and Okanagan were initially approved by Transport Canada for rapattack, and only the Bell 206, 206L-1 and 205A are certified for use. These are equipped with connecting points for rappelling ropes. Their skids are useful for the rappellers as they can climb out onto them before beginning their descent. Three rappellers and a spotter are normally carried. The pilot must be qualified and experienced, particularly in vertical reference work, a necessity when firefighters leave the helicopter from what is termed

*Logging debris—slash—can become a major fire hazard, so must be destroyed, in this case by controlled burning. The pilot of this Bell 206 (above) can ignite the mixture of gasoline and diesel oil fuelling the drip-torch with a solenoid activated from the cockpit. The liquid is burning when it drops onto the slash. In the 1980s, "ping pong balls" filled with a napalm-like substance were tried. These could be very dangerous for the helicopter crew, particularly in the event of a crash. (All, British Columbia Ministry of Forests)*

the deployment hover.

The rapattack system usually works well but has its limitations: in poor visibility, less than half a mile, operations are suspended, especially where the ceiling is less than 500 feet. With firefighters and their equipment suspended below the helicopter, rappelling is not carried out in winds of 17 knots or more. The helicopter could drift in such winds, possibly over the fire. Vertical reference flying is difficult enough without having to contend with dangerous winds.

*B.C. Forest Service crews at work. In the top photos a crew uses chain and compass to locate the sample plot, and the age of a tree in the sample perimeter is measured with an increment borer, a device which removes a small core containing the annual growth rings. The camp (lower left) has always been an integral part of life in the bush. No matter how rudimentary, it still looks good at the end of the day. (British Columbia Ministry of Forests)*

Setting slash fires by helicopter was also developed in British Columbia. In 1938 a serious fire broke out on Vancouver Island. The outbreak advanced rapidly in accumulated logging debris near Campbell River. It spread out of control over a 20-square-mile area, threatening Courtenay. Fortunately the town survived and the danger posed by slash (the debris of logging) resulted in constructive action. The British Columbia Forest Act had a section added (section 116) to ensure that the forest service could require the destruction of debris. This practice would help deprive a fire of fuel. Slash burning was normally carried out with hand-held Panoguns, devices similar to flame throwers which were fuelled with diesel oil. This was a time-consuming process and often required large crews.

In 1973 John Muraro of the Canadian Forest Service at Prince George developed what has been termed a drip torch: a 45-gallon oil drum bolted to a metal frame and connected to a long spout which dispenses a 60/40 mixture of diesel oil and gasoline. This apparatus is suspended below a helicopter and the fuel is ignited electrically by means of a solenoid activated by the pilot. The flaming liquid then drops to the ground, setting fire to the slash. Using the drip torch, slash burning can be more selective; it isn't necessary to fire the whole setting as would often be the case with ground-based methods, a process which could result in an uncontrolled fire and even soil damage. With the drip-torch operation, the pilot is directed by radio, sometimes setting a number of fires simultaneously. Using ground methods it would have taken perhaps 10 men to achieve the same result. There was also some element of risk to the ground crew; there is virtually none for the helicopter pilot.

While helicopters have proven so important in the protection and harvesting of British Columbia's timber resources, they have also been vital in a less exciting but equally important operation.

Forest inventory, a laborious process to determine the nature and extent of timber resources, has been going on for many years. But the introduction of helicopters in the 1950s made it possible to cover much larger tracts in the annual five-month inventory period. A helicopter could set out sample crews quickly. Usually a crew comprised two students who worked from a fly camp. They would hike from there to selected random samples marked on their aerial photographs. At their destination, they laid out circular plots about 60 feet in diameter, marked them off with orange seismic tape, and measured and described all the trees within them: the species, diameters, heights and ages —the latter on the basis of core samples taken with an increment borer. In this instance, the helicopter provided quick and economic transportation into remote and rugged terrain.

The helicopter was also used for forest classification or forest type description from the air. Before flying an area, a number of representative forest types would be selected from aerial photographs and connected to form a flight plan route. The route would then be followed, using the photographs to navigate from forest stand to forest stand, and the classifier, who was usually a graduate forester, would "call" the plots into a tape recorder, identifying the species and estimating the height, diameter and age of the trees. Classification was carried out just above tree-top level at about 40 mph. Data was checked from time to time by landing and allowing the classifier to compare his most recent "call" with actual measurements. If his estimates from the air had been faulty, he could adjust them accordingly. Information from each flight plan would be transferred from tape to classification sheets and correlated with the observed stands on the photographs after the flight. At the end of a season, all the data was brought together to produce forest cover maps.

An advanced approach to forest inventory, the helicopter-mounted camera boom, has been in use in British Columbia for more than 20 years. Hugh Lyons of the Ministry of Forests Valuation Branch was the first in the province to propose this method. He recalls: "The idea of the camera boom goes back to an article I was reading in *Photogrammetric Engineering Magazine* by Eugene Avery. He was working in the southern states and had experimented with a hand-held boom with two cameras, and had succeeded in

*Jack Gibbs (below) is shown securing the camera to this early version of the camera boom. This is the rear portion of the boom secured to the airframe of a Bell 47-G2. The camera was controlled from the cockpit (below right) by the apparatus being held by Hugh Lyons (above right). (British Columbia Ministry of Forests)*

*A number of attempts were made to determine the best method of mounting the camera boom. This Vancouver Island Helicopters Bell 47-G3B-2 (left) is shown lifting off with one version that was suspended from the airframe in an effort to reduce vibration. Ultimately (right) rigid mounting of the camera boom to the helicopter proved more effective than suspending it by cables. This type of boom was designed to be used with the Bell 206 Jet Ranger, in this case, a Vancouver Island Helicopters machine. (Both, British Columbia Ministry of Forests)*

getting measurements by laying out plots on the ground; in other words, using ground control. I talked it over with Bill Hall, the head of Aerial Surveys. So Bill and I figured that if you could get the cameras far enough apart, and knowing that the same distance would always separate centres, we felt that we could dispense with ground control.

"We then got hold of a couple of Fairchild F-24 cameras with five-inch film. Bob Taylor and I then put our heads together with Ron Adams who, like Bob, worked for Vancouver Island Helicopters. Ron built the first camera boom to my specifications. We mounted it on the helicopter by clipping it directly to the cross tubes below the cockpit and to the nose and tail by means of straps. This was necessary because there was a long cantilever.

"There was an electrical firing mechanism; wires stretched from the cameras on the boom up through the door into the cockpit and a control box. The system worked very well; accuracy was excellent. I was still looking for even better results, however. The cameras weren't fast enough and vibration was a problem.

"We then went to Linhof cameras to actually begin operation with the booms. Before this, all our efforts were purely experimental. There were still problems—the cameras wouldn't fire properly. If the rear camera fired too late or too early it would distort the base length. When things did work properly, it was possible to get accurate gross volume estimates of timber by species, and results were comparable with ground sampling methods. We checked this by flying a section with the boom and then checking the same area on the ground. We could get the same results for roughly 56 per cent of the costs experienced using ground methods."

The camera boom was progressively improved by the Forest Service. After the initial experiments with a fixed boom, which had resulted in vibration problems, a new approach was tried. A boom was produced which was attached by two lanyards to a longitudinal bar clipped to the cargo hook and suspended beneath the helicopter. This helped

*(Opposite) An important use of helicopters in the forests is aerial fertilization. The Bell 205 is having the bin of its dusting apparatus refilled. Time is an important consideration, so the helicopter simply hovers until the job is done. (British Columbia Ministry of Forests)*

*Helicopters are now used to collect cuttings (or scions) for breeding. Shears, operating off the helicopter's hydraulic system, are used to remove the cuttings. Before this method came into use, foresters would shoot scions down with a rifle, often using considerable amounts of ammunition and time in the process. (British Columbia Ministry of Forests)*

resolve the vibration problem, but the boom required a specific airspeed before it would fly without oscillating. Eventually, in 1976, another boom was designed specifically for use on the Bell 206. This system is attached by means of a semi-rigid mount to the helicopter in a matter of minutes and enables inventories to be carried out as an ongoing process over the six forest regions in the province. The use of helicopter-mounted devices has greatly simplified the work of the forest service, and in one case replaced a somewhat surprising tool of foresters: the rifle.

The forest service has for years been searching for what are called plus trees—trees that are as close to the ideal as possible—for each of the various species found in this province. By genetic engineering they hope to produce a super tree for each type that can be ''cloned'' to produce higher quality timber. This genetic information is acquired from cuttings, or scions, taken from the tallest, straightest, generally closest to perfect tree in a stand. Foresters on the ground would search out such trees and, using a rifle, shoot down a cutting. With helicopters, cuttings could be removed directly from tree tops by means of a harnessed crewman hanging out of the cabin. Before long, shears were developed to clip cuttings from trees, a device which worked off the helicopter's hydraulic system. Also baskets were developed to harvest cones so that trees no longer had to be climbed by pickers or felled so they could harvest the cones on the ground.

Helicopters have largely overcome many of the forest industry's problems associated with topography and geography, making possible and practical the harvesting, protection and inventory of near-inaccessible timber, and reducing dramatically the time required for routine forest management.

# Search and Rescue

*I do not speak English so good, but I know brave men, any*
*language, any country.*

GREEK SEAMAN: S.S. *Glafkos* Rescue, January 1962

Danger, whether due to rugged topography, darkness, dense forests or changeable and sometimes violent weather conditions, is often characteristic of search and rescue operations in British Columbia. In many cases the capabilities of a helicopter have meant the difference between survival and tragedy.

As early as 1943, the RCAF had attempted to acquire helicopters for rescue work. With the military flying in Canada during World War II, improvements were needed in the Air Force's rescue capability. Accordingly A/V/M E.W. Stedman, Director of Technical Services, requisitioned six Sikorsky XR-6 helicopters. This attempt, however, was thwarted by the federal Treasury Board, which insisted that costs were too high. The Air Force was to wait four years for the arrival of its first helicopters.

Canada took part in creating an important United Nations agency, the International Civil Aviation Organization (ICAO), when it held its first meetings in Chicago in late 1944. Subsequently it and other nations signed agreements committing themselves to set up standardized search and rescue facilities in areas where they exercised sovereignty. The organization of services in Canada was further refined on January 16, 1946, when the RCAF assumed chairmanship of an inter-departmental search and rescue committee to coordinate the efforts of all government facilities for search and rescue, including the Departments of National Defence, Fisheries, and Transport; and the Royal Canadian Mounted Police.

On April 5, 1947, the RCAF accepted its first Sikorsky H-5 helicopters, costs having been reduced by quantity production for the United States armed forces. The helicopter was to become part of a coordinated "team" of aircraft, ships and ground parties assigned to search and rescue.

When a search was necessary—a downed aircraft was among the most common incidents—fixed-wing aircraft such as Cansos, Norsemen and Lancasters would fly search patterns to locate the wreck and survivors. Pararescue teams would then be dropped along with survival supplies, and ground parties, where feasible, would hike in. Ground personnel would then prepare victims for removal to a point from which they could be evacuated. If it was a difficult situation, far removed from other forms of transportation, or one of great urgency, a helicopter would be used.

Ironically, perhaps, the first helicopter rescue in British Columbia did not involve the Air Force. In October 1947 an employee of the Greater Vancouver Water Board shattered his foot while working in the Rodgers Lake area of the North Shore. A North Vancouver doctor hiked up to the accident site. It was an arduous five-hour trek and, on assessing the problem, he recommended immediate evacuation. An attempt at removal using a Tiger Moth of Charter Flight Services failed. The topography immediately surrounding the head waters of the Capilano River prevented it from landing. Sheer rock cliffs rose to a height of 1600 feet on three sides, and frequent mists reduced visibility at that time of the year.

Jim Sampson of Aero Surveys Ltd., a division of Skyways of Winnipeg, was working in the vicinity. A mercy flight was arranged using his Bell 47-B3. In spite of heavy mist, he was able to fly up the valley and land on a sand bar that had been cleared of debris by Water Board workers. The injured man was loaded into the two-seat helicopter and flown to North Vancouver. With the assistance of police, a city boulevard was turned into a landing pad for the helicopter from which an ambulance took the victim to hospital. The 15-minute flight had made unnecessary an agonizing journey and a delay that might have had serious consequences for him.

In February 1950 a USAF C-47 search and rescue plane crashed into a western Yukon mountain while looking for a C-54 transport with 44 people on board thought to be down in the area. The C-54 had disappeared while on a flight from Great Falls, Montana, to Fairbanks, Alaska, on January 26. Once the wreck of the C-47 had been located, para-rescue teams, including a doctor, were dropped to care for the injured air crew. As soon as feasible, the survivors and rescuers were brought out to civilization by an Air Force helicopter. However, it had not been possible to evacuate them with safety directly from the 7300-foot crash site, so the entire party made its way on foot to a place where a helicopter could land and load. While under most circumstances the H-5 could use its rescue hoist to evacuate victims, the presence of stretcher cases made this impossible. The H-5 had to make nine trips, but it certainly demonstrated its usefullness. The C-54 transport was never found.

*British Columbia's heavily forested terrain makes locating a downed aircraft difficult. This 442 Squadron CH-113 has located a crashed Bell 47. (Canadian Forces)*

*The Sikorsky H-5 (S-51) was the first helicopter used by the Royal Canadian Air Force in British Columbia. It took part in Operation Brix, the search for a USAF B-36 in February 1950. The rescue hoist is situated immediately above the door. (Canadian Forces)*

Later that February, a USAF B-36 bomber of the 436th Squadron 7 BW(H) of the Strategic Air Command (SAC) experienced problems while flying south along the British Columbia coast from Fairbanks en route to Fort Worth, Texas. Distress messages were received shortly before midnight on February 13, indicating that severe icing was being encountered at 16,000-17,000 feet and that instruments were failing. Two of its six engines then caught fire and a third had to be feathered. The last message received suggested that ditching in Queen Charlotte Sound between the Queen Charlotte Islands and Vancouver Island was likely. Radioing from 90 miles southwest of Prince Rupert and over water, the operator made a final plea that searchers watch for flares or wreckage at sea.

Weather in the search area was poor. The ceiling was a mere 500 feet, and winds up to 52 mph were blowing, whipping up rough seas. Fortunately, surface visibility was better at three miles in light rain. But life rafts, assuming there had been time to deploy them, and especially life jackets, would be hard to spot even under favourable conditions. They would be mere "pinpricks" on the surface of the sea, obscured by rising and falling swells.

Aircraft from 123 Search and Rescue Flight, RCAF Station Sea Island, near Vancouver, were making their way north as soon as possible. RCAF search headquarters felt that the most critical search area would be along the last known flight path of the bomber, which led towards Vancouver Island over open water. The crew's chance of survival in the ice-cold water would be slim indeed and so time was vital. Hypothermia or exposure was the main worry, and it was possible that survivors in the water might drift apart. "Operation Brix," as the search was called, was to cover 25,000 square miles.

One aircraft making its way to the search base was the Sikorsky H-5 from Sea Island. Secured to a barge towed behind an RCAF tug, it headed up the Strait of Georgia. Because it was dangerous to fly a helicopter at night without proper instruments and training, this method was used to get as close as possible to the search area by daybreak when it

*Survivors of the February 1950 B-36 crash were taken to the Port Hardy search headquarters by a US Coast Guard Catalina amphibian shortly after their rescue from Princess Royal Island. They were quickly debriefed in an effort to discover what had happened and to get clues to the fate of the remaining five airmen. They never were found. (Vancouver Public Library 41228)*

was possible to fly safely. The helicopter lifted off from the tug on the morning of February 14, stopping off en route at the RCAF Station at Comox to have a mechanical problem corrected. It then flew on to Port Hardy, the forward search base.

Older helicopters were not the ideal search aircraft when little was known about the crash location. They lacked the range to cover large areas. Once the wreck or survivors were located, however, helicopters often could be the only means of rescue. They could also assist in directing ground parties or surface vessels to the site.

As it turned out the pilot of the B-36, after jettisoning his nuclear bomb, (which was never recovered) had turned towards land to give the crew a better chance of rescue. Twelve of the 17 crewmen were found on Princess Royal Island. The remaining five were never seen again; they probably came down at sea. Two U.S. helicopters joined the search and operated from the Surf Inlet area on the west coast of Princess Royal Island. After survivors had been located by ground rescue parties and some removed to the destroyer HMCS *Cayuga*, the Canadians were told politely but very firmly that it was now an American show. The presence of a nuclear weapon on board the bomber was undoubtedly the reason. When documents relating to the incident were declassified nearly 30 years later, it was learned that a "Broken Arrow," or nuclear accident, situation had been declared. The B-36 wreckage was not found until 1953, three years later, in the mountains south of Smithers.

In the rescue effort the helicopters were hampered by winds, poor visibility and darkness. Their small payload and short range had also restricted their value in this situation. Ideal in other circumstances, they were less than effective in this one.

In June 1950 a Rescue Coordination Centre (RCC) was established at the Sea Island Headquarters for No. 12 Group. All calls for assistance would now be passed through this agency, greatly increasing the level of efficiency and decreasing response time.

The H-5 went into a well-earned retirement as a rescue helicopter in British Columbia in the spring of 1955; its replacement, the Vertol H-21A, was introduced in March. The first of these large twin-rotor helicopters had been delivered to the RCAF in September 1954. Subsequently the H-21 was upgraded with gyroscopic stabilization, a feature which greatly reduced pilot fatigue. The H-21 had a medium-lift capability which made it much more useful than the H-5. It could carry greater loads internally and externally and do so

*(Opposite) The Vertol H-21A based at Sea Island was as impressive on the ground as in the air. Inflatable bags were attached to the landing gear for safety when operating over water. The cylinders attached to the folded bags contained the gas to inflate them. (Vancouver Public Library 4122)*

over a longer distance. These "flying bananas," so called because of their shape, were a great improvement.

H-21A 9613 had only been in service a short time when tragedy struck. On April 21, 1955, while on a routine flight from Vancouver to Cold Lake, in Alberta, it slammed into a mountain peak near Rossland. The pilot's vision had been obscured by blowing snow and fog while flying at low altitude, and he was unaware of the danger in his path. A witness related how the noise of an aircraft, followed by the sound of a crash, filled the cab of his truck. Only two of the five on board survived.

The lost machine was replaced by one of six ordered for the Mid-Canada Line. The new helicopter arrived at Sea Island in late December 1955.

On December 9, 1956, a four-engined Trans-Canada Air Lines North Star left Vancouver for Calgary with a crew of three and 59 passengers on board. Cleared to climb to 19,000 feet, it was already two hours late when it left the terminal at six o'clock that evening; weather reports received earlier hadn't been encouraging, indicating turbulence and snow.

At 6:57 p.m. the pilot reported to Vancouver that he had just lost number 2 engine in icing and extreme turbulence. Rather than continuing to Calgary, the pilot decided to return to Vancouver and requested permission to descend to 8000 feet, perhaps hoping to reduce icing at lower altitude. That was at 7:10. Ten minutes later, when the tower attempted to contact the North Star with landing instructions, there was no response.

There were three emergency airfields close to the plane's last reported position: Abbotsford, Penticton and Kimberley. When the plane was last heard from, it was, the pilot thought, just east of Hope, approximately 90 miles from Vancouver on Airway Green One of the Abbotsford Radio Range airways. It had enough fuel to last until 11:00 even if the pilot dumped his reserves, something he may have done if anticipating an emergency landing. The estimated time of arrival at Vancouver was 7:40, and when this passed and there was no indication that the plane had put down at an emergency field, there was concern. It was obvious that something was terribly wrong. The Rescue Coordination Centre launched two Lancasters from Comox, sending them to the airliner's last reported position. They were instructed to watch for distress flares or other signs of the missing aircraft. It was later reported that the plane was not carrying flares or any other emergency equipment beyond extra blankets—those on board would stand little chance of survival in this weather.

At first light, search aircraft began scouring a path 30 miles wide from the vicinity of Hope west to the Gulf of Georgia, a distance of about 100 miles. The search master, S/L George Sheehan, gave instructions that moutain peaks were to be checked closely and that aircraft should descend to even lower than 200 feet if possible, a dangerous thing to do in this region in these conditions. Visibility was poor and turbulence so severe that many aircrew suffered airsickness.

The searchmaster believed that the pilot may have become confused and gone off course, so numerous reports of flashes in the sky were checked out as were alleged sightings of wreckage. The Sea Island H-21A was kept busy but nothing was found. After 18 days the search was called off. Mountain peaks had been combed for wreckage by ground parties, especially Mount Cheam, 25 miles west of Hope, and Silvertip Mountain, some 18 miles southeast. The fate of the aircraft was a mystery.

In mid-May 1957, two climbers were making their way up Mount Slesse, miles from the other peaks searched in December, when they came across pieces of metal and clothing at the 7500-foot level. A metal part bearing a serial number was returned to TCA and subsequently identified as part of the doomed plane's fuel system. One of the reported flashes in the sky the night of the crash appeared to have been the North Star. An army

*When the wreck of the TCA North Star was located in May 1957, Mount Slesse became the focus of considerable activity. Officials from Trans-Canada Air Lines, the RCAF and the Department of Transport swarmed over the crash site. Here commercial helicopter crews are briefed by RCAF officers. (Eric Cowden)*

corporal from Chilliwack had seen a pinkish-orange flash near Vedder Mountain.

The searchmaster had been correct in assuming that the plane was off course: it was 30 miles from where it should have been and 50 feet too low. The plane had gone into the peak of Slesse and its wreckage was strewn over the saddle known to climbers as "The Circus." It was a difficult spot to reach, so helicopters were used to carry investigators and airline officials up the mountain.

The H-21A flew to the site to evaluate the situation after the discovery of the wreck, and other helicopters were on the scene as well. Bruce Payne, on his first job as a helicopter pilot, flew Bruce Young of the *Vancouver Sun* to the crash site. Young later wrote that "pilot Payne brought his craft onto the crash scene at exactly the same angle as the North Star must have taken in. It made my spine tingle to approach the spot even at 45 mph in a highly manoeuvrable helicopter." Helicopters carried parties headed for the wreck to the 5000-foot level from where they proceeded on foot. They then served as communication links between the radio-equipped parties on the ground and to keep the curious from the site. There was an inducement for people to attempt the hazardous climb—there were rumours that a passenger from the Orient, bound for the eastern United States, was carrying a money belt with $80,000 in cash. Two amateur climbers had to be rescued by helicopters.

Rumours had abounded in 1956 that the Royal Canadian Navy would soon be operating helicopters in British Columbia. The Navy had operated Bell HTLs (Bell 47s), Sikorksy HO4Ss (S-55s), and Vertol HUP-3s in eastern Canada off a platform-equipped frigate, the *Buckingham,* and off the icebreaker *Labrador.* The latter had made the difficult east to west voyage through the Northwest passage in 1955, using its HUP-3 and HTL-4 for ice patrol.

The Minister of National Defence, Ralph Campney, denied rumours that the RCN had plans to operate helicopters in British Columbia. It would, he felt, be redundant for that service to do so when the RCAF was already performing search and rescue as well as transport and communications duties with its helicopters. However, by 1958, VU-33 Squadron, RCN, based at Victoria's Patricia Bay Airport, was operating three of the HUP-3s. These machines were for utility work such as transportation and observation with the Navy's Pacific Command, but inevitably rescue became an important function as well.

The HUP-3, with twin rotors and single engine, was a design typical of Piasecki

*The HUP-3, shown landing at the playing field of HMCS* Naden *in Esquimalt, was powered by a single engine, despite its twin rotors. Three such helicopters were used for general duties with Pacific Command, Royal Canadian Navy, and on occasion carried out rescues. This HUP has been restored by the Pacific Vocational Institute and is now part of the Canadian Museum of Flight collection in Richmond, B.C. (Canadian Forces)*

the predecessor of Vertol and Boeing/Vertol. It was very stable and, though small, was robust—a U.S. military pilot had executed a loop in an earlier HUP in 1948. The HUP-3 had been designed as a "plane guard" for aircraft carrier operation. If an aircraft went over the side of a carrier, the helicopter would retrieve its crew. It was not amphibious, so had to rescue a downed pilot while hovering. The RCN machines, while not used in this role, occasionally used the internally mounted rescue hoist. The sling in these aircraft passed through a hatch in the floor through which the victim was hauled.

The use of the rescue hoist and sling invariably makes a two-man crew, apart from the pilot, necessary: one to secure a victim into the rescue harness, the second to operate the hoist and transfer the victim from the sling into the helicopter. This could make an H-5 or HUP-3 very crowded indeed. It was not long before the Navy was flying rescue missions and the hoist proved valuable, particularly in one incident near Victoria. A young mountain climber had suffered a fall on Mount Finlayson. Help was summoned and a helicopter from VU-33 was soon on its way. To reach the injured climber, a crewman had to be lowered to the ground to direct the pilot so that he could manoeuvre between the trees on the mountainside. The hoist was situated well aft of the pilot making visibility awkward. The fact that the victim had a spinal injury complicated things; he had to be moved as little and as gently as possible. Moreover, had good airmanship not been exercised the helicopter and its crew might well have been lost. As it turned out all went well and the climber was flown to hospital in Victoria.

In 1961 RCAF Station Sea Island was deactivated and 123 C & R (Composite and Rescue) flight moved to Comox, the main RCAF base in British Columbia. Comox, 150 miles north of Victoria, was home to 409 Interceptor and 407 Maritime squadrons. It was more centrally located for coastal rescues, a factor that was to prove important in future operations.

In January 1962 a Greek bulk carrier, the *SS Glafkos,* was heading for Vancouver to take on a cargo of grain for Venezuela. Working its way along the west coast of Vancouver Island, it went off course, and high winds pushed it towards that rugged coast that had claimed so many ships over the years.

Hard aground at Amphitrite Point south of Barkley Sound, the *Glafkos* presented one side to the shore, the other to the sea, too far from the shore for a rescue via breeches buoy, a lifesaving line from shore. The wind was far too strong to permit an attempt from the weather side.

The Island Tug and Barge Company of Victoria dispatched salvage vessels to the scene and the Rescue Coordination Centre ordered the 121 C & R helicopter into the air. It was to land two salvage experts and their equipment on board and remove most of the crew. Several plates on the bottom of the ship's hull had been ripped off by the rocks holding the vessel fast, and it was taking on water. Without power, there was no hope of using the ship's own pumps. The priority for the helicopter became to sling two portable pumps on board. This was soon accomplished.

*In January 1962 the 10,000-ton Greek cargo ship* Glafkos *lost power and ran aground on the west coast of Vancouver Island. High winds pushed the ship onto the rocks and made it unlikely that a rescue could be made by a lifeboat or a line from shore. An H-21A from Comox was despatched to lift endangered crewmen from the ship and place salvage experts and their equipment on board. (Maritime Museum of British Columbia/Elworthy Collection)*

*The Vertol H-21A and Grumman SA-16B Albatross were the mainstay of search and rescue work until the introduction of amphibious CH-113 Labradors. The large number of marine incidents in British Columbia requires amphibious aircraft for SAR. (Canadian Forces)*

A *Colonist* reporter, Ed Cosgrove, hired a Vancouver Island Helicopters' machine to see the *Glafkos* first hand. He arrived just as the big Vertol was moving in. In the Thursday, January 4, issue of his paper he recorded his impressions: "We watched breathless as the RCAF helicopter edged closer to the stern of the ship which lay broadside to the sea and wind. . . . Precise as a hummingbird the big twin rotor machine dropped to wave top level and wished its way up to the stern of the wallowing freighter.

"Man after man dangled for nerve tingling minutes over the tossing sea. The helicopter would flutter shoreward returning minutes later for another man."

With most of the crew safe on shore, the ship's anchor cables were cut and the *Glafkos* was pulled free under supervision of the salvage crew and towed to Victoria. Had a helicopter not been able to place the salvage crew on board and remove the seamen, the ship and several lives would almost certainly been lost. The Vertol H-21A's performed their assigned roles very well for several years but they too were replaced before long.

In October 1963 search and rescue on the West Coast was upgraded by the introduction of the Boeing/Vertol CH-113 Labrador helicopter. The new machine had twin rather than single engines and was amphibious.

In late July 1963, F/L D.M. Campbell, flying a CH-113, was involved in a rescue that earned him the Air Force Cross. A civilian aircraft had gone down on a Vancouver Island mountain slope. An attempt to winch the survivors out with the hoist failed as the line was too short. With daylight fading, Campbell allowed the helicopter to settle onto the tree tops. A rescue team climbed out of the Vertol down the trees to the ground, and prepared the survivors for evacuation. Campbell later returned to lift the whole party out. Once again he was forced to execute the dangerous landing on the trees. Experience proved crucial and a difficult rescue was accomplished.

*A 1978-vintage Canadian Forces CH-113 SAR helicopter of 442 Squadron, CFB Comox, is seen on a training exercise. Note its searchlight, bubble windows, and long-range fuel tanks (rear sponsons). Further mods have since been added, including nose radar. (Canadian Forces)*

On occasion helicopters have been instrumental in evacuating people on a large scale. In January 1966, during one of the worst winters on record, slides in the Fraser Canyon cut rail traffic between the coast and points east. The eastbound *Panorama,* a Canadian National transcontinental passenger train, became stranded by slides at Stout, 20 miles north of Hope. It could move neither forward nor back. An Okanagan Bell 204-B airlifted food for the passengers and train crew, landing on a makeshift pad near the train. A second Okanagan machine, a two-seat Hiller 12E, was chartered to carry CN officials over the site to plan their strategy.

Plans to extricate the train by January 9, two days after it had been marooned, appeared unworkable. With fuel for the train's steam heaters running low, it became necessary to remove the passengers. The railway contacted the Rescue Coordination Centre and a Labrador was very soon on the scene, working along with the Okanagan Bell 204-B in the evacuation of 209 persons. By the end of the operation, the Vertol, according to Air Force sources, had removed 184 people.

On July 8, 1968, in another reorganization, 121 C & R Flight became 442 Squadron.

By mid-1976, Ottawa was at last convinced that air-sea rescue should be improved. In November it was announced that four mothballed helicopters would be returned to service. They were Army Voyageurs which, having been built as tactical transports, required major conversion to upgrade them to rescue configuration. Comox was to have its complement increased from three to five machines.

The conversion program, Search and Rescue Capability Update Project (SARCUP), was still under way in the spring of 1982. One aircraft from Comox was back at the Boeing Vertol plant at Arnprior, Ontario, for upgrading. Four helicopters will be on hand at all times until the conversion process, upgrading and mid-life refit are complete. The program is scheduled for completion by 1985.

The hoist on the Voyageur is in the midship position; it extends through the floor as in the HUP-3. It will be moved to the door on the forward part of the starboard side. The pre-conversion position of the hoist created problems for pilots since visibility towards the rear was limited. According to Lieutenant Colonel Gordon Diamond, in 1982 Commanding Officer of 442 Squadron, "It's like sitting at the front of a boxcar and attempting to watch what's happening behind and below you. Pilots must depend on mirrors mounted on each side below the nose and upon directions from crewmen to position the aircraft when making a hoist rescue. This situation was particularly difficult when a pick-up was being made from a vessel in heavy seas—the wildly gyrating masts can give the helicopter crew some bad moments since the hoist line can become fouled in the rigging or the helicopter itself may be struck."

The Voyageur was less sophisticated in its original configuration than the specially built Labrador, which had from the beginning been intended for search and rescue. Most subsystems are hydraulic on one aircraft, electrical on the other. The two machines are almost totally incompatible in terms of parts—over 2500 components are different—even though externally they look the same.

Pilots in 442 Transport and Rescue Squadron, the sole West Coast military SAR unit, are specialists either in fixed-wing or in rotary-wing aircraft; few fly both types. Their fixed-wing aircraft are Buffalos. It takes a minimum of 500 hours helicopter time on type for a pilot to be considered for command of a Vertol, which carries a crew of six: two pilots, two SAR (Search and Rescue) technicians, and two engineers. The Buffalo also carries a crew of six: two pilots two SAR technicians, a flight engineer and a navigator. The SAR technicians, a fairly recent trade classification in the Candian Forces, are trained paramedics, scuba divers, bushmen, parachutists and moutaineers. These people have the satisfaction of being the ones who actually effect the rescue.

The Buffalo, with its superior instrument flight capability and navigator, will often act as a "pathfinder" for the helicopter, particularly in the case of missions out to sea. The extension of Canada's territorial waters to 200 miles expanded the area of responsibility for Search and Rescue as well. An important aspect of the Voyageur upgrading was the enhancement of its range by increasing fuel capacity; the two sponsons at the rear of the machine were replaced by larger Kawasaki-built tanks. When an incident occurs far out at sea, the helicopter, even with improved range, can waste little time on site. With the Buffalo providing navigational aid, the rescue can be made more efficiently and with greater safety.

The two types are therefore complementary in the search and rescue role. The Buffalo has superior range, speed and altitude, so it more useful in medevac (medical evacuation) operations from distant locations, while the helicopter is the better machine for operating in a restricted space. Often both types fly together, particularly where little is known about the emergency; for example, when an ELT (Emergency Locater Transmitter) signal is received. An ELT is set to transmit signals automatically by the impact of a crash, and aircraft with direction finding equipment can home on the signal. The Buffalo, when it has homed in on the signal, can drop flares if the incident occurs at night, lighting the search area, and the helicopter is equipped with "Night Sun," a searchlight mounted below the nose. The two-million-candlepower light is useful once the location of the victim is known more precisely.

The Rescue Coordination Centre at Canadian Forces Base Esquimalt, near Victoria, is responsible for 690,000 square miles of water and 310,000 square miles of land and water—for a total area of one million square miles. It extends north from the Canada/United States border, to cover all of British Columbia, the Yukon, and the Northwest

Teritories west of the Mackenzie River; and out to sea for 200 miles and east to the Alberta border. The nature of the territory covered creates problems. Mountains and valleys can make the accurate locating of an ELT signal difficult because the signal can bounce off the valley walls for a considerable distance. In one incident, a signal from an ELT was picked up in the Enderby region of the Okanagan. As is standard procedure, a Buffalo and a Vertol were quickly airborne to locate the aircraft and determine the problem. As it turned out, the signal had come from a plane at the Spokane, Washington, airport—the topography had carried the signal north. Weather conditions can be and often are difficult, creating severe problems. Rescue aircraft are often called to operate in far less than ideal weather—in conditions which have often been a major contributing factor to the original problem. Regardless of the weather, certain procedures are always followed. Lt. Colonel Diamond describes a typical operation:

"In the case of an aircraft being reported as overdue to the Rescue Coordination Centre, several things happen almost simultaneously. The Department of Transport undertakes a communications search to determine if any messages have been received from or concerning the aircraft. The RCMP or other available agencies will check airstrips along the last known flight path of the plane—by phone if possible, or in person if no phone is available. In the meantime, we usually launch both a Buffalo and a helicopter with full crews —which are in the air less than 30 minutes of the call from the RCC.

"The first day is critical since there may well be injuries. We maintain a constant watch for signals over the next two days and nights, and comb hills along the flight path. When the RCC message is received, I'm informed and, along with the squadron operations officer, appoint a search master. This is usually a captain on the squadron who has been fully trained in this role, and an assistant. A search master has a big job, directing the operation of what can sometimes be 60 or 70 aircrew and spotters. During the winter months, he's usually up at 0600, in the summer 0500, preparing his search strategy, maps and briefing packages for crews. When the aircraft return to refuel, he will interrogate the crews and give them their assignments for the next phase of the search. Assisting the search master will be an accounts clerk with a 'bag of money' to pay for hotels and food, and people to provide for the logistical end of the operation—fuel and maintenance for the aircraft, and communications. He must be left as free as possible to direct the search. One other complication is dealing with the press, relatives of the missing, and on occasion, politicians. A search can last any time from a few hours in some cases, to days or weeks in others. Some are successful; some are not—it's a matter of luck as well as skill.

"One prolonged operation in which I was involved within the last year [1981], was the search for an Air B.C. Beaver that had gone missing on a flight from an Indian village at Klemtu to Ocean Falls with some federal government employees on board. We searched along the flight path normally taken by Air B.C. aircraft without success, but spotted an oil slick on the surface of a lake. Using a blotter, we took a sample of the oil—as you can appreciate, it was thin and difficult to collect. The first sample was insufficient but the second worked and we sent it to the RCMP crime lab for identification. The oil proved to be of a type similar to that used by Air B.C. in their aircraft.

"The next step was to dive on the object releasing the oil to determine if in fact it was the Beaver or simply a piece of equipment that may have fallen off a barge at some point. Where there is some possibility of saving life, we would normally send in our SAR techs who are qualified scuba divers. Such was not the case in this instance and the object was in any case far too deep. We contacted CanDive who sent down a sonar device and determined that the object was metal, man-made and of an angular shape, not unlike that of a Beaver aircraft. In order to be certain, however, it would be necessary to dive using a small submersible. We were fairly certain that we had found the aircraft but had to be sure. Two Hercules transports were sent down to Houston, Texas, where the CanDive sub was working. We nevertheless continued the air search and, shortly before the C-130s were ready to return with the submarine, one of our spotters saw the wreck of the Beaver in an area we had flown near perhaps 15 times before. Hidden in high timber, it went in without having broken a twig. We were fortunate to have found it. Apparently the Beaver had run out of fuel a mere eight miles from its destination. Unhappily, the pilot and passengers were all dead.''

Not all searches are as extensive as the one just described. In late August 1976, a Comox-based Labrador flew three separate missions in one day. The first was fairly routine, picking up an injured hiker in the Buttle Lake region of central Vancouver Island; the second was to Wolfe River, some 20 miles into Strathcona Park. At this point things started to go wrong. While evacuating a woman from a heavily forested area using the hoist, everything went smoothly until the woman ''became excited'' and damaged the hoist. The account does not elaborate about how this occurred. Later that day, they were sent out for another evacuation to the Forbidden Plateau ski slopes near Comox. The helicopter developed a vibration which forced the pilot to land on an access road. A truck from base arrived with parts and maintenance personnel and the helicopter was soon on its way again to pick up an injured skier and return to base. It had been a long day.

The duties of 442 Squadron are varied, including search and rescue, humanitarian missions such as emergency medical evacuations—though this type of mission has declined with the creation of a provincial air ambulance service—and giving aid to the civil power, such as assisting in the control of penitentiary inmates, flood control and forest firefighting. Incidents involving lost or downed aircraft have been constant over the past decade, but those involving pleasure boats or larger vessels have increased dramatically. Most incidents are routine, but there are some that are spectacular. One of these involved the *Prinsendam,* sailing in the frigid North Pacific.

At 2:25 a.m. Pacific Daylight Time, October 4, 1980, Victoria Marine Radio monitored a distress signal from the Holland-Amerika Lines cruise ship *Prinsendam,* at sea 150 miles west of Sitka, Alaska. Twenty minutes after the ''mayday,'' the duty controller at RCC Victoria reported the situation to the duty operations officer at 442 Squadron, CFB Comox, in case any aircraft might be needed quickly. RCC Victoria had immediately offered assistance to its counterpart in Juneau and was asked by them to stand by; a Search and Rescue aircraft was on its way to the scene to look things over.

The first report from the ship had indicated that the engine room of the 430-foot vessel was on fire. The fire spread rapidly and soon the ship, dead in the water without the use of its engines, had flames shooting high above the decks. The situation had become desperate. Two and a half hours after the first mayday, the 329 passengers and all of the crew except those fighting the fire were ordered into the lifeboats. Some of these lifeboats, designed to carry 50 persons each, had as many as 80 crowded into them—a necessity since two others were unusable because of problems with the lowering gear. The passengers, virtually all of whom were dressed in sleepwear, had no protecton from spray, wind and cold; what had started as a leisurely cruise from Vancouver to the Orient had turned into a nightmare.

RCC Juneau requested that the Canadian aircraft and crews be prepared to leave at one and a half hours notice. Staff at Victoria RCC, by now certain that they would become involved in the rescue, recalled Labrador helicopter 11306 from a medical evacuation to Vancouver, and requested 442 squadron to prepare additional aircraft and crews to assemble as soon as possible in support of RCC Juneau. The anticipated request came at 6:15 a.m. Helicopter assistance was required at the scene and fixed-wing aircraft were

*Responding to the* Prinsendam *distress call in October 1980, Canadian and American helicopters and fixed-wing aircraft operated in very poor conditions. Here, a Canadian helicopter with its "night sun" searchlight in operation is approaching a lifeboat. (USCG)*

*Survivors from the* Prinsendam *were taken by helicopter to the USCG Cutters* Boutwell *and* Mellon, *and the tanker* Williamsburg. *A Coast Guard HH-53 is shown approaching the landing pad at the stern of the* Mellon. *The* Boutwell *before long had 87 on board, including two Air Force pararescue personnel and the occupants of a lifeboat that had temporarily gone missing in the deteriorating weather. (USCG)*

needed for transport duties. A rescue force was already converging on the stricken ship and her passengers.

An American supertanker, the *Williamsburg,* had responded to the *Prinsendam's* call for assistance and was standing by, as was a US Coast Guard cutter, the *Boutwell.* No time was wasted; American helicopters were already transferring survivors from the boats to the *Williamsburg* and the pad-equipped *Boutwell* even before the arrival of the Canadians. The tanker, with a crew of only 29, quickly found itself overwhelmed.

Two Labrador helicopters and two Buffalos were dispatched from Comox as soon as they were fuelled and the crews briefed; an additional Buffalo left the following day. A main function of the fixed-wing support was to transport the considerable equipment and personnel related to both rescue and salvage operations to Yakutat and then on to the *Prinsendam* and, later, those passengers and crew of the ship who required hospital treatment, between Yakutat and larger centres with more extensive facilities. An Argus maritime patrol aircraft of VP 407 Squadron also headed north from Comox to act, along with an American Hercules transport, as a communications link and rescue watch for the Canadian aircraft and US Coast Guard and Air Force helicopters from Sitka, Kodiak and Elmendorf.

The nearest point to the rescue with an airport, Yakutat, was the logical base for receiving survivors. With the cooperation of the Alaska state authorities and the citizens of the town, the considerable preparation required was carried out successfully: a Command Post and Reception Centre were established in the airline terminal and the high-frequency radio was set up in the airport manager's office. Limited contact with search headquarters in Juneau was maintained by a landline. Aircraft operating between the ships and shore used Yakutat as the base. Major C.B. Fletcher, Acting Commanding Officer of 442 Squadron, was asked by Juneau to take charge there until a USCG replacement could arrive.

Canadian Forces medical personnel, as soon as possible after their arrival at Yakutat, were on their way to the *Williamsburg.* Master Corporal R. Holliston, Team Leader, reported later that "there were approximately 100 survivors on board, and we were the only medics available. We checked all the survivors, completed emergency treatment, and set up an area in the main mess deck to check and treat new survivors coming aboard."

Captain Gary Flath in Labrador 11303, which had taken off from Comox at 7:51 a.m., arrived at Sitka some 800 miles to the north at 1:25 p.m. Nurse Captain Costello remained at Yakutat where she would be needed when evacuees began arriving in large numbers.

The weather was beginning to worsen, and Captain Flath, after refuelling, was bound 20 minutes later for the *Williamsburg* carrying six medical personnel: three Canadian SAR technicians, Molly Seifert and Anne Keinitz, both trained paramedics from the Alaska Civil Defence organization, and Major McLean, Base Surgeon at CFB Comox. The tanker proved difficult to locate and Flath requested that the ship transmit so he could home on it without visual contact. Seifert was on board Flath's Labrador for the trip to the ship. Recalling the incident, she wrote:

"1:30 p.m. My first ride on one of these and am not sure how I'll react, but what a ride! The weather is getting worse all the time, with winds increasing and raining steadily, and I can't see where we're going.

"2:30 p.m. We figure we'll be on the tanker within 45 minutes. Someone mentions a fire in a helicopter and I'm checking exits! Not to worry, the helo that left before us has an electrical fire and may have to ditch, so we circle a couple of times. The pilot gets word that another plane is escorting the first one to Yakutat.

"We land on the tanker *Williamsburg*, which is doing quite a dance on those seas. We slip and slide over what seems like miles of pipes and ramps, etc., to get to shelter. Another discovery—the helo pilot hasn't landed on a ship before!"

Meanwhile, Captain Ken Pettman, who had left Sitka in Labrador 11306 just as Flath in 11303 had arrived, was coping with technical problems. Everything had been functioning normally en route to Sitka and for the first portion of the trip out to sea, but before long, things began to go wrong and Pettman was forced to declare an emergency. Navigation systems had failed and attempts to have Argus 731 home in on the helicopter proved futile. The Emergency Location Transmitter (ELT) was turned on and Flath indicated that he could home on the signal if necessary. This proved unnecessary since a USAF C-130 was able to locate the helicopter and was in formation within two minutes of the declaration of the emergency. Captain Pettman, by this time feeling utterly frustrated at having come so far without problems, only to have to turn back, asked that the Hercules escort him the 120 nautical miles back to Yakatut, where they arrived safely at 4:50 p.m.

After unloading on *Williamsburg* and hearing that Ken Pettman was being escorted back to base, Flath headed for the *Prinsendam*, which he reached some five minutes after lifting off the tanker. A lifeboat was located, one with only 40 persons in it, and the decision was made to use the high line and the horse collar. This was the fastest method of recovery in such severe wind and sea conditions. Before long, passengers were being hoisted into the aircraft. A "Sky Genie," a rope normally used by an SAR technician when he descended from a hovering aircraft, proved to be an effective means of returning the horse-collar to the boat after a survivor had been hoisted into the aircraft.

As Flath recalls: "The Sky Genie rope remained attached to the hook and collar, with Sergeant Williams holding onto the other end of the rope. This enabled me to move the aircraft off to one side to allow better reference on the boat during recovery, and to keep oscillations of survivors being hoisted to a minimum. When the hook and cable were being let out I could stay clear until I saw Sergeant Williams hook up another survivor. I would then move over the boat and, as the cable tension was tightened up, would lift up gently on the collective when directed by the hoist operator. This manoeuvre ensured that the survivors cleared the boat quickly to avoid getting wet or caught up on the lifeboat."

Fifteen people were removed from the first boat by Flath's helicopter and flown to the *Williamsburg*. A further 16 people were removed from a second boat with Master Corporal Lang being lowered to the boat and Master Corporal Amadio working the hoist.

Meanwhile, on board the *Williamsburg*, medical personnel and crew attempted to cope with exhausted, cold and frightened people. Tired and short of medication, clothing and space, the "medics" began to feel the strain. As Molly Seifert described the scene: "Into the night the paramedical personnel meet each other coming and going throughout the ship's living quarters. We all make rounds of all four decks, stopping to visit with people who can't sleep, carrying coffee, sandwiches, etc.

"3 a.m. to 5:30 a.m.: We all sit and drink coffee with the two Canadian paramedics. If the lady rescuers look as bad as the guys, there'll be no contests won. I think I would kill for a shower and a Coke."

There were still more passengers to be removed from the boats. Flath, with his Labrador, continued hoisting people and at one point looked for a lifeboat that had gone missing. The cutter *Boutwell* requested that the helicopter attempt to find the boat so, very short of fuel, Captain Flath trimmed for endurance flying. "The weather was very poor at this time, with 100- to 200-foot ceiling, and 1/2 mile visibility and high winds which made it very difficult for rescuers to spot the white lifeboats hidden by large swells

*After the passengers and crew had been removed from the* Prinsendam *and the fire extinguished, the stricken vessel was taken in tow by a British Columbia tug,* Commodore Straits, *for the long trip south to dry dock. The Dutch liner never made it to port, capsizing and sinking at 3:30 a.m. on October 11 in 9000 feet of water. (United States Coast Guard)*

and whitecaps. When the cutter finally saw me I flew over the lifeboat and flashed my landing lights. Once he acknowledged that he had a visual on the lifeboat, I departed for Yakutat and arrived there 1.5 hours later, after dark, with about five minutes fuel remaining.''

With the last survivors located and safely transferred, the rescue vessels headed for Valdez. For Molly Seifert it had been an exhausting but memorable experience: "It will take a good two weeks to get this out of our systems. After flying home on a Canadian Air Force Buffalo, Anne and I spent almost two hours mostly staring at each other. My family got the doubtful privilege of being sounding boards. My immediate reaction was to try to tell everything that happened and we both talked and laughed and related war stories until we were hoarse. Ironically, very few people in Sitka knew we were gone. It is difficult to come to the realization you are part of a history-making event, at best; and when no one knows you were there being a hero, it becomes impossible.''

Attempts to salvage the *Prinsendam* and return it south for repairs failed when, under tow by the Vancouver-based tug *Commodore Straits,* the ship capsized and sank in 9000 feet of water. The rescue itself was extremely successful, more than proving the value and effectiveness of the search and rescue organizations involved. All the passengers and crew had been lifted off safely and remarkably quickly, considering the distance from shore. Without the helicopters and other aircraft, the rescue would have been far more difficult and lives might well have been lost. As ever, cooperation between Canadians and Americans involved was excellent.

The United States Coast Guard was a very early operator of helicopters; they were quick to appreciate their advantages in search and rescue work. In November 1943 the USCG set up a training base for helicopter aircrew at Floyd Bennett Field, New York, where pilots for that service, the Royal Navy and the US Navy were trained on Sikorsky R-4 helicopters. The first helicopter mercy mission flown by the Coast Guard took place in the first week of January 1944 when Commander Frank Erickson flew plasma to treat victims of a ship explosion. He had to fly the desperately needed supplies in bad weather from New York to Sandy Hook, New Jersey. While it was not a long flight, it did dramatically demonstrate the value of helicopters in such circumstances and began a long tradition of helicopter rescue work by the Coast Guard.

The US Coast Guard Air Station at Port Angeles, Washington, some 20 miles south of Victoria on the Strait of Juan de Fuca, received its first helicopter in 1950. This was a Sikorsky H03S-1G like the H-5 used by the RCAF at Sea Island. Before this, the rescue service had employed a variety of fixed-wing aircraft such as lifeboat-equipped Boeing PB1G (B-17) Flying Fortresses from the Ediz Hook base, and even after the introduction of rotary-winged craft a number of flying boats and amphibians such as the Grumman UF-1G Albatross continued to operate from the station. The helicopter was quickly pressed into service rescuing victims of marine and aircraft accidents and carrying out medical evacuation missions. The role of helicopters in search and rescue has changed little in terms of the type of operations flown but their capability has increased dramatically due to advances in techniques and, obviously, technology.

The US Coast Guard, like the RCAF, replaced its aircraft when those of superior capability became available. Sikorsky H04S-2G helicopters, the Coast Guard/Navy equivalent of the S-55 used by Okanagan, were introduced in the early 1950s. In October 1956, the USCG had occasion to call on the Canadian search and rescue service for assistance. Two USAF Northrop F-89D Scorpion jet interceptors had disappeared from radar over the rugged Olympic Mountains and it was vital that the aircrew be located as quickly as possible. It was feared the pilots might have come down high in the mountains where, at high altitude during winter conditions, exposure could prove fatal. That was assuming they had survived the crash. A very large area had to be searched.

The Rescue Coordination Centre at Sea Island responded immediately, sending an Otter fixed-wing search aircraft and a Vertol H-21A helicopter. Since it was possible that the airmen might have come down in the Strait, the RCC also sent four tugs of Island Tug and Barge Ltd. of Victoria to the scene. Apparently when one of the F-89Ds had developed technical problems, the second had moved in to have a look and the two aircraft

*Medical evacuations—medevacs—are almost routine for SAR helicopters. This HO4S from the USCG Air Station at Port Angeles, Washington, is shown waiting to load an accident victim for the trip to hospital. (USCG)*

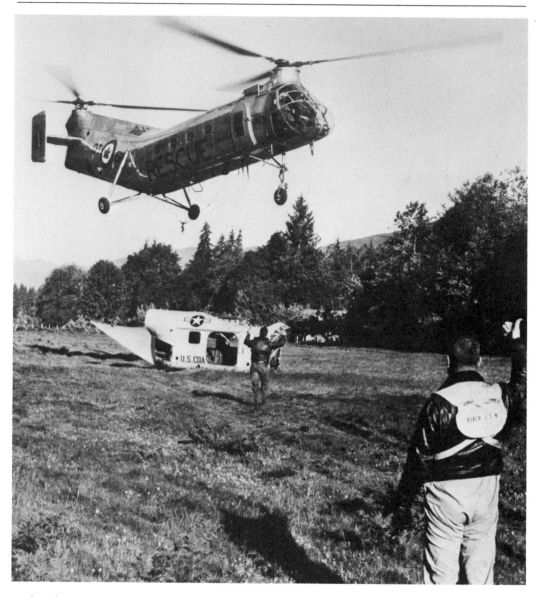

*Reduced to its "essentials" with its engine, cockpit, tail boom and rotors removed, this Coast Guard HO4S was salvaged by a Sea Island H-21A in October 1956. The American machine had gone down in a white-out. Damage was light enough to warrant salvage but too severe to permit it to be flown out. (USCG)*

had collided. Three of the four crewmen ejected successfully and parachuted from the aircraft, which crashed three miles from each other on the west side of Humes Glacier. The *Vancouver Sun* reported on October 6, 1956, that two of the aircrew had been located by RCAF aircraft—one by the H-21A and the other by the Otter. The first survivor was rescued by the Vertol, and the second by a Coast Guard HO4S helicopter, which had been directed to the site by the Otter pilot. The third survivor was able to walk 40 miles out to safety.

One of the USCG helicopters crashed during the search operations when it encoun-

*No longer used by the USCG by the mid-1970s, a "horse collar" is being used to hoist a "survivor" off a pleasure craft in this training exercise near Port Angeles. (USCG)*

*This platform simplifies the job of getting a frightened, possibly injured, survivor into the aircraft. (USCG)*

tered white-out conditions. Fortunately the crew were uninjured and the helicopter was not a write-off. It could not be flown out, however, because the damage was too severe for repairs to be carried out on site; weather conditions and logistics would have rendered this difficult in any case. The obvious solution was an airlift by a large helicopter. Fortunately the RCAF Vertol was nearby and it had the capacity to do the job. The downed HO4S was stripped; the engine, cockpit and tail-boom were removed to reduce weight, and the H-21A airlifted all the pieces out for repair and reassembly.

In 1963 the Sikorsky HH52A single-engined, amphibious helicopter entered service with the US Coast Guard. It could operate off water and reduced the dependence on fixed-wing amphibious machines to deal with the large number of marine incidents characteristic of northern Washington and southern British Columbia. Ensign Jeff Vail, who

*Ensign Jeff Vail, USCG, (left) and Lieutenant-Commander Denny Maclean, USCG. (USCG)*

has served as a co-pilot on the type, describes the duties of a copilot and other aircrew:

"When the SAR alarm goes off, you respond quickly: while the Aircraft Commander goes out to pre-flight the aircraft and run it up, the co-pilot gets all the details he can on the case and then runs to the airplane. My job when airborne is to do a few checks and handle the radios, the onboard computer, and to navigate while the Aircraft Commander is doing the flying. He usually makes a decision, informs me and I pass it along to the base. If it's a particularly difficult mission, he'll fly the airplane, but sometimes we'll swap, otherwise you'd get no experience flying. I usually monitor the radios and the aircraft's in-flight performance. I'll also act as an observer.

"On a standard SAR mission, we normally go with a three- or four-man crew: one man is a dedicated flight mechanic and it's his job to maintain the helo between missions. A lot of his training for rescue work centres around hoist operation. On a search, he acts as an observer. He may or may not have paramedical experience, and so we try, if possible, to take a duty corpsman along with us, particularly in the case of a heart attack. Any aviation 'rate'—aviation mechanic, avionics tech or in fact anyone involved with the aircraft—can become qualified as a SAR aircrewman and go out on a mission. Anyone who works with the aircraft can qualify.

"We seldom, if ever, drop an aircrewman to assist with a rescue, since both our aircraft and crew are too small for that. Perhaps it's the type of flying we do; we spend a minimum time on site because the helicopter simply doesn't have the endurance to remain for any length of time. We no longer use the 'horse collar,' except in cases involving trained military personnel; the Coast Guard dropped that since too many people were slipping through—one of the astronauts almost drowned while being hoisted in one a few years ago after a mission. We use the basket and the Stokes litter."

In a situation which often involves a high degree of risk in the normal course of operations, the rescuers can on occasion end up on the receiving end of rescue efforts. Just such a situation occurred in early 1976. Commander Paul Milligan relates what happened: "It was February 29, 1976, a memorable day apart from being a leap year. It was sometime after midnight and I'd only just drifted off to sleep when the phone rang—one of our aircraft was down while responding to an emergency on the west coast of Vancouver Island. We didn't know a thing beyond this and the fact that the weather was extremely bad, with intermittent snow and heavy winds, which made the situation particularly difficult. Getting to the base in what must have been record time, we launched immediately and headed for Cape Beale where the incident occurred. Even from our side of the Strait, we could see that a Canadian SAR aircraft was dropping flares.''

Lt. Commander Dennis Maclean, then a lieutenant, was flying as co-pilot on this mission and subsequently served on the board of enquiry. He relates details of the incident: ''We soon learned by radio that a Canadian Coast Guard 44-footer [Bamfield Lifeboat, CG-104] had picked up our crew and two survivors of a fishing boat, and that all were well. Knowing this and having no desire to fly under flares while they were being dropped, we flew to Neah Bay where we stayed the night. The next morning, in beautiful clear weather, we headed for Cape Beale to pick up our crew and investigate the loss of the airplane.

''We learned that the H52 had been in the vicinity of the Cape Beale lighthouse the night before on another call—the Canadians would have normally handled it but couldn't get over the mountains separating Cape Beale and Comox in the weather—when the lighthouse keeper contacted them by radio. He had heard cries for help but couldn't locate their source. Our crew, from the air, spotted someone clinging to the reef in the vicinity of the lighthouse and were able to make a hoist rescue. Almost as soon as the survivor was on board the helicopter, there was a loud bang and the pilot instinctively pushed down on the collective to autorotate onto the water—probably on instruments under the circumstances.

''Safely down, he still had to contend with heavy seas and snow, and winds of 30-40 knots. The helicopter was in immediate danger of being pushed onto the rocks and pounded to pieces. The water was too deep for an anchor to be effective and so he deployed a sea drogue, a device not unlike a small parachute. This became fouled around the sponson and was ineffective. By this time, the aircraft was rolling from side to side—it was a miracle that it was still afloat at all since it had not been designed to cope with seas of this magnitude. Half the length of each rotor blade was disappearing below the surface of the water with each roll. It was obvious that it was going to be necessary to leave the aircraft. The crew spent a nervous 20 minutes in the pitching, rolling helicopter edging towards the rocks, until a Zodiac boat, launched from the Canadian Coast Guard 44-footer, came alongside to take them off. Knowing what had happened, the lighthouse keeper had directed the Canadian 44-footer in through the reefs using a CB radio: 'Go left, go right, back up'—that sort of thing. Once the drenched helicopter crew and the boat survivors were below and warming up, a crewman told them that they weren't safe yet—they still had to get out the way they had come in, once again using directions from the lighthouse keeper to clear the reefs. The bottom of the boat scraped over the reef at several points.

''When we looked at the remains of the H52 the next day, the largest piece that we could locate was the bottom of the hull; the fuselage above the level of the floor had been completely sheared off. The first part we went after was the engine. After investigating, the conclusion we came to was that snow had been ingested into the intake and the 'fire' had gone out.''

The crew of the Bamfield lifeboat, Coxswain David Christney, and crewman Martin and Clifford Charles, and Robert Amos, were presented with a Certificate of Commendation by the Commissioner of the Canadian Coast Guard in a ceremony on March 6, 1976. This was in recognition of an ''outstanding rescue at sea . . . under extremely dangerous conditions, demanding the utmost skill, courage and devotion to duty in the finest traditions of the sea.'' The US Coast Guard too presented an award to the lifeboat crew and lighthouse personnel.

Generally speaking, the presence of the amphibious HH52A helicopters near Victoria has proven vital on numerous occasions but perhaps never more so than a foggy day in

128

*An Air West Twin Otter similar to the one referred to below. (Robert D. Turner)*

December 1976. An Air West Twin Otter, a twin-engined STOL aircraft equipped with floats, was approaching Victoria on a late morning flight from Vancouver when it ran into heavy fog. The harbour, with its marine traffic, can be difficult even in good visibility so the pilot elected to put down at sea and wait until the weather cleared enough to enter the harbour safely. The aircraft hit the water at 110 mph and bounced 150 feet into the air. The impact damaged a float and the plane began to settle to one side shortly after it landed.

A mayday distress call went out immediately. The Rescue Coordination Centre at Esquimalt responded quickly, requesting assistance from the US Coast Guard at Port Angeles, only 20 miles from the crash site. Within 16 minutes of the distress call, an HH52A landed beside the sinking plane. It was 11:34 a.m. All 16 passengers and the two aircrew of the Twin Otter were quickly taken on board the US helicopter. Then, without warning, the plane tilted and a wing moved up into the rotor arc of the HH52A, shearing pieces off the rotor blades. The damaged helicopter had to be towed back to Port Angeles. Crash victims, all of whom were in good condition thanks to the fast action of the Americans, were transferred to a Canadian pilot launch for a quick trip into Victoria and waiting ambulances. Praise for the US helicopter crews was heartfelt. A CTV news cameraman, who was on board the Twin Otter, commented that if it had not been for the USCG he thought it unlikely that he'd have been around for Christmas, which was only eight days off. While this incident, like many others, had a happy ending, such has not always been the case.

In September 1980 a US Navy HH46A from Whidbey Island Naval Air Station responded to a call from the Esquimalt RCC to rescue an injured hiker. By the time the helicopter reached Perfect Pass, near Vedder Crossing, flying conditions were marginal, with scattered clouds below 8000 feet and a solid overcast. To complicate matters, it was only 30 minutes until sundown and they were still about 30 miles south of their destination. Lt. Richard Wall, USN, the co-pilot, was doing the flying while the pilot and a sheriff were checking maps. A new heading was decided upon and control of the aircraft was transferred, the Aircraft Commander turning the helicopter to the new course. Suddenly, without warning visibility was lost and the radio altimeter indicated that the ground was coming up fast. They had lost 1600 feet in just four seconds, and just as the altimeter reached 400 feet the helicopter crashed.

Lt. Wall was thrown clear of the wreck and 200 feet down the side of the mountain. He was very fortunate; five of the seven on board the HH46 had been killed; only the deputy sheriff and he survived. Late in the morning following the crash, two hikers arrived on the scene and, performing what first aid they could, made the crash survivors as comfortable as possible. Leaving their packs, water canteens and warm clothing, the hikers went for help. The next day, rescuers arrived. Richard Wall describes what happened:

"At first light the next day I felt a wave of emotions like none before or since, as I heard the sound of an H-46 [CH113] overhead. The clouds were in solid, but the Canadian HH46A crew from 442 Rescue Squadron, Comox, British Columbia, gave it their all. Hovering IMC [Instrument Meteorological Conditions], with only a few rocks for reference, the Canadian crew commenced the rescue in weather worse than at the time of our crash. I recall thinking, 'Lord I hope they know what they're doing!' and apparently they knew just that, as the rescue proceeded without a hitch and we were flown out to the nearest hospital."

Both Richard Wall and the deputy sheriff recovered from their injuries. This incident vividly demonstrates the dangers encountered in rescue missions by American and Canadian crews. Cooperation between the rescue services of both nations has always been excellent since they share the same traditions that have characterized individuals and organizations dedicated to the saving of life. The helicopter has proven to be all that its inventors could have hoped in this respect.

*Introduced into USCG service in the early 1960s, this HH-52A based at Port Angeles is lowering a rescue basket, standard hoist rescue equipment, into Seattle Harbour. Inflatable air bags attached to each sponson are inflated in the event of an emergency landing at sea. Though amphibious, the HH-52A is not designed for long periods on the water. A Stokes litter (left) is standard equipment on rescue helicopters. With it, a survivor can easily be hoisted into the helicopter. Here flotation gear has been added as a precaution. (USCG)*

# CHAPTER 10

# Canadian Coast Guard

*After some time, we spotted the boat in a vast expanse of
ice, looking like a black speck on a white sheet.*

BOB JONES

Canadian Coast Guard experience with helicopters began in 1950 when a Sikorsky S-51,
CF-DOY, was acquired by the Marine Service of the Department of Transport, the predecessor of the Coast Guard. Jack Charleson, Canada's first civilian to qualify on helicopters, had suggested a year earlier that a helicopter operating from a deck rigged on
the "fan tail" of a ship would prove useful in ship-to-shore transportation and ice patrol
duties. Flying helicopters off ships had been tried before; in May 1943 two Sikorsky R-4s
were successfully test flown off the tanker SS *Bunker Hill* in Long Island Sound. There
had been proposals earlier to use ship-based rotary-winged craft in an anti-submarine
role and with later developments they have excelled in this military role.

Charleson's suggestion was put to the test and, despite an accident which destroyed
the S-51—a tie-down cable from the deck of the vessel to one side of the aircraft had not
been detached before take-off and the helicopter crashed—the Department of Transport
was more than satisfied with helicopters and purchased a number of Bell 47s over the
years to service lighthouses and other marine navigation aids, and for use with East
Coast icebreakers and buoy tenders.

Initially they were used almost exclusively from ships, their primary roles being ice
patrol and personnel and light cargo transport. In the early years all the helicopters were
based at the Air Services headquarters in Ottawa and were detached to the various
marine agencies when requested. This worked reasonably well when only a few ships
were equipped with flight decks. The success of helicopters in these roles tended to
obscure their potential as land-based transport. It was in the latter role that helicopter
operations began on the Pacific Coast in 1960 when two Bell 47G-2s were based at Vancouver and, a year later, a larger Sikorsky S-62 began flying out of Prince Rupert.

In British Columbia, as on the East Coast, the primary purpose of the Department of
Transport Marine Services was the maintenance of coastal aids to navigation, still a vital
task today on this treacherous coast. Ships had to be protected against natural hazards
such as reefs and against each other. Spare parts and technicians could be airlifted to
sites where repairs were required on short notice and the construction of helipads near
navigation aids from 1961 onwards dramatically reduced the time required for resupply
and maintenance. These functions had previously been carried out using ships such as
the lighthouse tender CGS *Estevan.* The introduction of the aircraft had a morale-
boosting effect of the personnel at lighthouses: they were less isolated. If an emergency
were to occur, if someone were sick or injured, it was possible to carry out an evacuation
quickly. Though the value of the helicopters was proven beyond doubt, their efficient use
was restricted to a degree by a bureaucratic complication.

The basing of the two Bell 47-G2s in Vancouver proved to be inefficient because the
main Department of Transport Marine Services base in the province was then, as is that
of the Coast Guard now, in Victoria. Both machines and air crew were the responsibility
of Air Services, and their use by Marine Services had to be formally requested—a cumbersome and illogical practice. For almost a decade the helicopters were exclusively land-

based in British Columbia. The inefficiency of this situation became apparent when operations from icebreakers recently equipped with landing-pads began in the late 1960s. Ivor Roberts, a long-time Coast Guard pilot who had received his initial training on Sikorsky R-4 helicopters with the Royal Navy shortly after World War II, explains the situation:

"We started out servicing the lighthouses—there are about 30 in this agency—from the Vancouver side. They would bring the helicopter over from the hangar there and work off two icebreakers; one was the *Camsell*, which we still have, and the other the *Simon Fraser*, which is now back in Quebec. There were no facilities here in Victoria until they got an office and space in one of the old Fairey hangars [Fairey Aircraft of Canada] which we kept for some years. We then went to the VU-33 hangar when they abandoned it and stayed there until we got our facility at Ogden Point. We were always divided in our loyalties between Air Services and Marine Services and this situation continues even to this day, since administration is by Air Services and for operations it's under control of Marine Services."

Administrative problems notwithstanding, the role of West Coast helicopters expanded dramatically with the construction of flight decks on two Victoria-based icebreakers. These ships had been constructed in British Columbia yards to service Distant Early Warning Line radar sites in the western Arctic from the West Coast.

As had been the case in Eastern Canada for some years, the helicopters before long were used for ice patrol from the ships on the annual northern re-supply cruises. Sailing from Victoria, usually during the first week of July, the ship proceeded west and north, passing through the Aleutians at Unimak Pass, and stopping at the US Naval base at Dutch Harbor to refuel if the ship was not accompanied by a tanker. This base was one

*Canadian Coast Guard Bell 47-G2s carried considerably more radio equipment than their commercial counterparts. Bob Jones is at the controls in this mid-1960s photo. (CCG)*

*Des O'Halloran at the
controls of a CCG Bell 47-G2.
(Des O'Halloran)*

of the few locations on continental North America attacked by the Japanese during World War II. From there the ship passed into the Chukchi Sea and the northwest passage. Once through the Bering Strait, the ship passed Point Barrow into Cambridge Bay and finally into Spence Bay, the last point on its voyage.

The helicopter provided the "eyes" for the ship when it was making its way through the ice, an important job since it is all to easy for even an icebreaker to become trapped. The *Camsell* found itself in those circumstances in 1979 when its hull was holed by pack ice and the engine room flooded. Fortunately the ship did not sink and it was returned to Victoria for extensive repairs. Bob Jones, who has flown 10 seasons in the north with the Coast Guard, describes the procedure employed in ice patrol work:

"The helicopter normally scouts 20-30 miles ahead of the ship, carrying an ice observer who makes a detailed map of the ice field for the ship's captain. Nowadays they have a complete division of ice observers, and they put one on all the ships carrying helicopters. The ice observer's job is to give a picture of the ice amount and type; you have, say, 8/10 of ice of which 3/10 is polar and 5/10 pack ice. Polar ice is usually relatively easy to go through unless you have some that is rafted (that is, new ice piled on top of old). Polar ice is refrozen year after year and there's no limit to its thickness—it can be anywhere from 5 to 150 feet thick.

"Single-year or winter ice normally poses little problem for the icebreaker, but multi-year or polar ice can, and often does. It can damage both icebreakers and other shipping. Sometimes when the ice is particularly bad, the helicopter will literally lead the ship through 'weak spots' by hovering only 100 yards ahead. Usually in these circumstances, a ship's deck officer accompanies the pilot, as he will be better able to decide on the ship's capability of penetrating the ice ahead.

"The other major problem associated with the ice is determining whether or not it is under pressure—that is, pressure from wind. Any ice field under pressure can bring all but the most powerful icebreakers to a halt. Once the wind abates, however, normal navigation is resumed. Where ice fields are extensive, the helicopter would be on patrol at intervals of two or three hours. Knowing where the thicker, more difficult ice is allows the ship to take the 'path of least resistance' through the field."

Weather conditions in the Arctic are generally good during the summer, with constant daylight or at least twilight. There is, however, occasional fog and the possibility of whiteout, when an overcast sky and the snow merge without any discernible horizon, making visibility difficult or impossible. This is extremely dangerous when flying, and

*Pilots had to exercise care in landing on floating ice because the weight of the helicopter could cause the ice to roll over without warning—or, on larger areas of decaying ice, the helicopter could break through, the jagged ice cutting its floats. This Coast Guard G2 had canvas covers to protect the floats. (CCG)*

particularly unpleasant according to Jones since "you lose your horizon and of course your sense of balance becomes shaky. You do everything possible to avoid such circumstances since the instrumentation on the helicopter is inadequate for such conditions."

On board ship, the helicopter is stored in a telescopic hangar extended by means of cables operating a rack and pinion on each side of the hangar. In other words, the hangar can be extended to cover the helicopter when it is on its landing area on the deck, then retracted for takeoff. This is a tremendous improvement over working on an exposed flight deck as had been the case earlier. The structure provides an excellent working space for the engineer, as Ian Duncan recalls: "You've got steam heat in the hangar and we had our own compressed air system for cleaning parts or whatever you wanted to do. We also had our own facilities on board. When we first started all we had was barrels, 45-gallon drums, which was a dangerous situation. With the addition of the hangar, there were always two seamen assigned to the engineer to help out on the flight deck—such as getting the machine in and out."

On occasion, though, the combination of a warm hangar and a machine in which vital components were exposed could result in potentially serious problems. Once again in Ian's words: "The only trouble we did have was going ashore to one of these bases. You'd take the aircraft out of this heated hangar, and if there was any water in any part of the lower cables, like your throttle, just as soon as you got airborne this water would freeze. On this occasion the throttle froze. We got ashore okay and we stayed at the base for about half an hour. But when we came out we still couldn't move the throttle.

*The telescoping hangar on the* Camsell *can be rolled aft to cover a helicopter on the pad or remain folded to clear a larger area of the deck for operating the helicopter. (D.N. Parker)*

The only way I could thaw it out was to get a little propane torch and just lightly dust it over the cable.''

The Bell helicopters used on board the ships were much like their commercial counterparts with an open latticework tail boom and exposed engine and fuel tanks and tail-rotor shaft. The main difference was the amount of radio equipment carried. Compared to most helicopters in use today, the G2 was less than sophisticated. According to Bob Jones, ''the Bell 47-G2 was the last machine which you were literally flying by the seat of your pants—since there was no slip or drift indicator, your 'seat' told you if you were flying correctly. Fixed-wing instructors always said to keep your 'nose' on the horizon. Try doing that while enclosed in a plastic bubble.'' Despite its limitations the 47-G2 was for several years the Coast Guard workhorse.

A typical day for the helicopter crew would, in addition to the ice patrol, involve transporting personnel to shore—it was faster and less dangerous to do it with the helicopter. The icebreaker carried a doctor who would go ashore to visit facilities and settlements as part of the routine health service. He would even extract teeth if necessary. In addition to these routine duties, the helicopter crew would on occasion assist Eskimos who had experienced difficulties. Bob Jones recalls one such incident:

''Working among Eskimos for many years with the eastern and western Arctic Patrols, one finds that they have many distinctive characteristics. Generally a happy people, they rarely go into shock, and adversity is accepted as a normal part of life. An example of the latter occurred in 1972 when on patrol in the Rasmussen Basin. It was a bad ice year, the thaw late in coming, and the winter ice extended almost shore-to-shore. We had a message from the settlement of Gjoa Haven on King William Island asking us to

*The Canadian Coast Guard's big S-61N, seen in November 1979 at Vancouver. Its home base is Prince Rupert. (Brent Wallace)*

and landed and I saw this old girl come over the fence and it was just going to land when the engine failed again—just quit dead. He [Bob Jones] was about five feet off the ground and he just autorated down and landed safely.''

The defect was to remain a mystery, at least to the people concerned. The engine was returned to the manufacturer and no word was ever received, or at least passed on, as to what the problem was.

In January 1972 Coast Guard Sikorsky S-61N CF-CGF, which had replaced the S-62 with the Prince Rupert agency in the late 1960s, experienced mechanical problems on a flight north from the lower mainland with 10 people on board—ice had been ingested by the engines due to the absence of a shield. The pilot was able to make an emergency landing on Triple Island in Hecate Strait. The people were rescued and plans were made to recover the large aircraft. It was situated too far from the shore to be retrieved by means of a barge and crane, so it was decided that it would be brought out by air.

A Canadian Forces Labrador from 442 Transport and Rescue Squadron, Comox, the only machine available with the necessary capacity, was pressed into service. With everything possible removed from the Sikorsky to reduce weight—engines, rotor, instrumentation and radios—the recovery operation went ahead. The wind increased in velocity and the stripped helicopter fuselage suspended below the Labrador began to "fly" on its own. The Labrador pilot had no alternative but to punch it off. The S-61 was written off and replaced in 1973. The replacement, also an S-61, was equipped for IFR (instrument flying) capability. As had happended earlier, rumours abounded, and were denied, to the effect that the Coast Guard would be undertaking some responsibility for rescue.

The Coast Guard Air Service does not include search and rescue among their responsibilities although the Rescue Coordination Centre has on occasion requested the assistance of their machines. Coast Guard hovercraft and rescue cutters, however, do have a vital role to play. While they are almost exclusively concerned with the maintenance of aids to navigation, the whereabouts of Coast Guard helicopters is known at all times should an emergency occur in their location. The Canadian Armed Forces have the primary responsibility for search and rescue and are equipped and trained accordingly. If the rescue services were increased, it would make more sense to expand existing facilities than to create a new organization. The Coast Guard, because its name is similar to the United States Coast Guard, is mistakenly attributed with having the same powers and responsibilities, and equivalent aircraft and equipment.

In addition to its tasks on coast waters, the Coast Guard services navigation aids, all of which are unmanned automatic facilities, on northern inland waters using Victoria-based aircraft and aircrew. The entire Mackenzie River, from its source to its mouth, is marked. The Bell 212, a twin-engined development of the 205 produced for the Canadian Armed Forces, and designated by them as the CUH-1N, carries out the medium-lift assignments, usually working the Mackenzie River and Great Bear and Great Slave lakes during the early part of the season. Well liked by its crews, the Bell 212 has more power and capacity than the Alouette, as well as a much greater range. In Coast Guard configuration, it can carry nine passengers: five forward and four facing each other. The normal commercial configuration carries four more in space taken up by extra auxiliary tanks on the Coast Guard machine. With the 212, it is possible to carry three or four technicians, with their tools, equipment and supplies, to service three or four lights on one trip. After the heavier work is completed, an Alouette or Bell Jet Ranger rakes over for the 212, freeing the larger machine for service in British Columbia once more. The Jet Ranger, a light helicopter, is an ideal aircraft for the ice patrol and usually goes north with the *Camsell* on its annual voyage.

## Royal Canadian Mounted Police

The Royal Canadian Mounted Police have operated Bell 206 Jet Ranger helicopters in a variety of roles since September 1973. Before the, commercial operators were frequently called upon to provide machines for emergencies. Helicopters have made possible a rapid response to such situations as bank robberies or prison breaks, providing aerial observation posts to coordinate and direct ground units. Evidence from a crime site can be transported by helicopter directly to the RCMP crime laboratory in Vancouver.

*Shown in July 1981, shortly before joining the icebreaker* Camsell *on its annual northern resupply cruise, this Victoria-based Bell 206 replaced the Bell 47s on ice patrol. (D.N. Parker)*

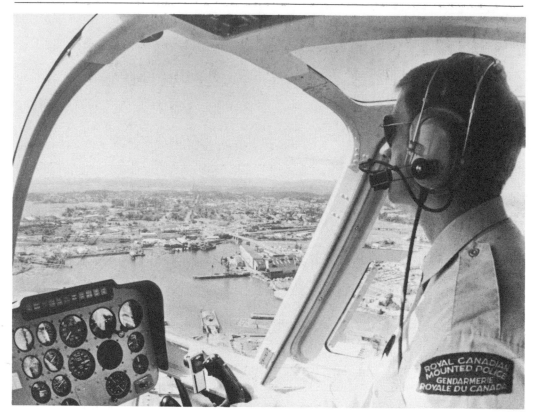

The Royal Canadian Mounted Police acquired their first helicopter on the West Coast, a Bell 206 Jet Ranger, in September 1973. Tom Vickers is shown at the controls over Victoria. (Provincial Archives of British Columbia/Jim Ryan Collection)

In late June 1984, WM Aviation of North Vancouver demonstrated the Aerospatiale Dauphin II, which it hoped to use on a Victoria-mainland scheduled passenger service. (D.N. Parker)

# In Retrospect

Immediately after the Second World War, when helicopters began to appear in public, the media, egged on by the manufacturers, extolled them as the ultimate vehicle. They could rise vertically (everyone assumed with a full load), hover motionless, move sideways or even backwards—there was nothing a helicopter couldn't do and confident predictions were made that within a few years there would be a helicopter in every carport.

Yet in 1947, when the helicopter was first introduced into British Columbia, the technology was in its infancy as were the techniques for flying the new aircraft. It lacked the performance to achieve what the dreamers expected of it and, given both its virtues and its shortcomings, operators lacked the experience to market it effectively. Consequently helicopter operators had to develop techniques to overcome the "myth" of a helicopter's potential, and replace the myth with realistic expectations.

Experimentation was the answer. Companies like Okanagan and individuals like Carl Agar, who risked his life to develop mountain flying techniques, made British Columbia one of the most significant regions for helicopter use in the world. Potentially useful roles for the helicopter that didn't work out—crop dusting was found to be unfeasible at least in the Okanagan—were quickly discarded, while others, such as search and rescue, forest fire fighting and power-line construction, were persevered with and developed.

As helicopter operations increased, new equipment, much of it developed in British Columbia, was introduced: monsoon buckets for forest fire suppression, drip torches for slash burning, and camera booms for forest inventory and evaluation. Helicopters were, by the mid-1970s, pulling old growth logs off otherwise inaccessible sidehills; transporting foresters, geologists, surveyors and biologists to worksites; maintaining aids to coastal navigation; carrying out search and rescue and medevac missions; and acting as flying cranes in construction and industry.

The future may well see the start of offshore drill rig resupply operations like those on the east and Arctic coasts, an increase in the amount of scope of military flying and probably greater use of helicopters by corporations and the media. A scheduled intercity helicopter shuttle service seems likely to remain economically impractical for some time; and the other dreams of the forties—a helicopter in every garage, for example—never will materialize because of the complexity and cost of the technology (can you imagine the accident rate in crowded city skies if the average driver could move vertically as well as horizontally?).

Helicopters have by now assumed an important role world wide. In British Columbia particularly, with its rugged terrain and vast distances, their contributions and those of the people who have operated them have been particularly outstanding. But perhaps the most persuasive evidence that helicopters have arrived was provided recently when a charter launch sank in Hecate Strait, just south of the Queen Charlotte Islands. Twenty people abandoned the launch and took to two rubber dinghies. Four hours later, bobbing around in 20-foot waves, they were winched up into Canadian and US Coast Guard helicopters. The media, on this occasion, made very little comment about the helicopters; they had come to be accepted as run-of-the-mill rescue vehicles. The magic may have faded from the public consciousness but the value, in a case like this, is practically beyond a price tag.

# A Brief History of Helicopter Development

With the first successful flights of their "Flyer" in December 1903, the Wright brothers proved that powered, heavier-than-air flight was possible. But their solution to the problem of flight—the airplane—did not entirely fulfill the dreams of visionaries and experimenters of preceding centuries. The hope, and indeed the expectation, of these early aviation enthusiasts had been that man would someday be able to control his movements in the air just as he could on land or sea. The conventional airplane—one which needs forward momentum to fly—can neither take off nor descend vertically, nor can it hover. However, the elements of a machine that can—the helicopter—have existed for centuries.

Evidence from as early as the fourth century B.C. exists of a helicopter-like toy in use in China. It was a simple device. A short rod or stick was surmounted by a cork into which four feathers were inserted, each placed at right angles to its neighbour and "canted" or raised along one edge. When the shaft was twirled, the toy would rise into the air. As further proof of their antiquity, similar toys have appeared in paintings with children dating from the 15th century, and types are in use today.

Archimedes, the Greek mathematician, physicist and theorist of the second century B.C., developed a machine which inspired the 15th century artist and engineer Leonardo da Vinci to design a helicopter. Archimedes produced a type of screw which, enclosed in a tube and turned with sufficient speed, would raise water, a duty it has performed to the present day. These devices irrigate agricultural land in the Middle East.

Da Vinci correctly deduced that air reacted like water and that the screw device developed by Archimedes would therefore logically be able to make its way through air as well. This was provided that the tube enclosing the screw were removed and the speed of rotation increased to compensate for the lesser density of air. Da Vinci's design for a helicopter or "helix," as it has been called by others, appeared in a 1505 manuscript. He wrote:

> If the instrument made with a screw be well made—that is to say of linen which the pores are stopped up with starch—the said screw will make its spiral in the air and it will rise high [and he went on to explain that] when force generates swifter movement than the surrounding air, the air becomes compressed after the manner of feathers by a sleeper. And the thing which drove the air, finding resistance in it rebounds after the manner of a bell struck.[1]

No indication is given as to a power source. Likely da Vinci was simply testing the theory of a screw operating in air. It is uncertain whether or not he actually flew even a model. Power was to remain a problem in flying until an engine was designed that was both light and powerful. However, the famous scientist did not view this as a problem: in the case of at least most of his flying machines, he believed that man, with his great strength compared to that of birds, would be able to fly with ease if only he had a suitable machine; but he had misunderstood the manner and means by which birds fly. These principles were not understood until, in 1670, Giovanni Alfonso Borelli produced a book entitled *De Moto Animalum,* which proved that man's power-to-weight ratio was insufficient for flight. Borelli demonstrated that man was too weak and too heavy, and lacked the appropriate muscles to fly. This realization was to limit experimentation.

The only successful investigation into helicopters until the 20th century was very limited and carried out with models. They could be powered easily in reduced scale, but the springs or bow-strings used would hardly have been practical for full-sized machines.

In 1754, Mikhail Lomonosov, known today within the Soviet Union as the "Father of Russian Science," demonstrated a helicopter device in model form before the Russian Academy of Sciences. Called an "Aerodynamic" by Lomonosov, it was "to be used for the purpose of depressing the air by means of wings rotated horizontally in the opposite directions by the agency of a spring of the type used in clocks in order to lift the machine into the upper layers of the air."[2] The model was intended primarily to carry test materials aloft in the course of other experiments. Scientists, however, who have become interested in the helicopter as such foresaw a different application.

In 1768 a Frenchman, J.P. Paucton, in his *Théorie de la vis d'Archimedes,* described a machine capable of vertical flight—a "Pterophere." It was impractical, but Paucton is remembered as the first to suggest that a helicopter could carry a man. The English, not to be outdone, also began investigations into the problems of vertical flight. In 1796, 30 years after Paucton's experiments, Sir George Cayley, who was later to become known in Britain as the "Father of Aerial Navigation," turned his attention to a model that had been produced in France. Launoy and Bienvenue, respectively a naturalist and mechanic, had built and flown a similar device before the French Academy of Sciences in 1784. After some study, Cayley was able to improve the aerodynamic qualities of its airscrew, making it more efficient. This exercise marked the beginning of his investigations into the performance of airfoils—wings.

In 1799 Cayley developed the theory of the separation of lift and thrust—two of the forces working on an airfoil—and within a decade, by means of a whirling-arm test device, that of streamlining and the changes in the centre of pressure of an airfoil. John Smeaton, the famous civil engineer, had inspired this investigation with his work on the effects of wind speeds and pressures on windmill vanes. Cayley, unlike da Vinci, had the advantage of being familiar with Borelli's work; and understood how birds fly. He appreciated the fact that feathers at the tips of the wings rotated as they beat the air.

The pace of technological progress and experimentation accelerated in the 19th century, and with it came refinements which would ultimately lead to powered flight. Robert Taylor, an Englishman living in the United States, and correspondent of Cayley, had become intrigued with a marine propeller invented in the 1830s by John Ericsson, the Swedish-American naval engineer, and wrote to the English inventor in 1842. Taylor felt that the marine propeller could be adapted to flight and that construction of a vertical lift machine was feasible. He wrote that the machine he proposed would

> resemble an immense flat umbrella—the power and weight situated at the handle—the stem being hollow or double shaft revolving contraiweis [sic] when the vanes, of which the top is composed, are inclined, in ascension. The propeller or ''compeller'' is situated a little below the centre of gravity . . . .
> The lateral movement of a large plane surface edgewise to attain and retain altitude is, I conceive, your original invention or idea. I divide the plane which is circular into fourteen vanes: eight susceptible of inclination in one direction, and six (the lower or inner series) in the other direction.
> The rotary or ascensive action could be dispensed with if sufficient speed were attained by the rotary propulsive action with a general angle of the whole machine; but to start from the ground requires a perpendicular ascent, at first, and I consequently screw the plane up.[3]

There is a distinct similarity between Taylor's proposal and an 1843 design published by Cayley in *Mechanic's Magazine.* Both would seem to favour rotary wings—rotors—to raise their machine vertically. In Cayley's aircraft, these flying surfaces would then have the blade pitch reduced so as to function as wings in forward flight. The design reflected the English inventor's earlier work in that the rotor's blades were slightly cambered and given an angle of attack. Rotors on one side of the aircraft would turn counter to those on the opposite side. This neutralized torque—the force which would otherwise turn the body of the aircraft in the same direction as the rotor—and the gyroscopic action which would invariably roll the machine over to one side. The design prepared by Cayley was at the concept stage—had he tried to build a full-sized working aircraft, problems would have quickly become apparent.

Cayley and Taylor would have experienced difficulty in designing the mechanism to drive their creations. A steam engine, the best power source that contemporary technology could provide, would have been too large and heavy with its boiler firebox, fuel and water. Cayley knew this and suggested that an internal combustion engine might be the answer:

> It may seem superfluous to inquire relative to a first mover for aerial navigation, but lightness is of so much value in this instance that it is proper to notice the probability that exists of using the expansion of air, by the sudden combustion of inflammable powders or fluids with great advantage.[4]

But a practical engine of that kind did not exist and attempts by other aircraft designers made use of existing types of power plants.

Models employing tiny steam engines were flown in 1863 by the Viscomte Gustave de Ponton D'Amecourt of France, and in 1878 by an Italian, Enrico Folanini. The Frenchman is often cited as the first to use the term ''helicopter,'' in a patent of 1861. His model featured two coaxial contra-rotating rotors —turning on the same shaft—and a small steam engine. Unfortunately, it didn't work. The patent that D'Amecourt was granted in Britain in 1861 reads, in part, ''The required ascensional motion is given to my aerostatical apparatus (which I intend denominating aeronef or helicoptere), by means of two or more superimposed horizontal helixes combined together.''[5]

The United States in the 19th century was a fertile environment for the inventor and inevitably several turned their efforts to developing vertical-lift aircraft. One American proposal would have avoided the necessity of carring a steam generating plant aloft. In 1849, J. Henry Smith envisaged a machine which he felt would be ideal for military purposes. Steam was to have been supplied by a long hose connecting a portable boiler on the ground to an engine situated directly below a rotor. An umbrella-like parachute was mounted above the rotor for safety in the event of an engine failure. The machine would, however, have been uncontrollable in any but the vertical mode and would have provided little or no advantage over balloons.

A New Yorker, W.J. Lewis, built and allegedly flew a model helicopter in 1876. It used two rotors, which looked much like horizontally-mounted sails, to raise it into the air and others, vertically-mounted, to propel it forward. Wings attached to the roof of

AYRES NEW AERIAL MACHINE.

The May 9, 1885, issue of *Scientific American* carried this artist's conception of a vertical-lift aircraft designed by a Professor Ayres. Compressed air was to fill the frame, and power for the rotors was to be provided by foot pedals. The pilot would have had his work cut out for him.
*(Scientific American)*

the passenger cabin were intended to provide lift in level flight. While a small clockwork motor proved to be sufficient to power the model, the inventor intended the full-sized version to be powered by foot pedals.

The May 9, 1885 issue of *Scientific American* contained an illustrated article describing an aerial machine designed by Dr. W.O. Ayers of New Haven, Connecticut. Though the main driving force was to be compressed air under 3000 pounds pressure, foot pedals were to assist in raising the machine via two horizontal "fans." The propellers were quite small but could be enlarged. It was necessary to experiment, in the inventor's opinion, to determine how large they would have to be and the speed with which they would have to be turned. Controlling the aircraft, which had its tubular steel frame filled with air for lightness, was fairly straightforward: "Thus far we have only two motions, vertical and horizontally direct: but our apparatus must be steered precisely like a boat, and it must ascend and descend obliquely."[6] In this imaginative design, elevators and rudders are basically flat plates intended to operate much like the control surfaces of an airplane. It would apparently take off nearly vertically without "ground roll."

There was no shortage of would-be helicopter inventors during this period, but the problems of power and control made all their dreams impossible. There were many potential applications for a small, lightweight engine, however, and with all the experimentation going on in the 19th century, it was inevitable that someone would succeed.

As mentioned, Sir George Cayley had suggested that some form of internal combustion engine might be the answer. Some means by which a piston could be forced to move within a cylinder other than by steam pressure had to be developed. Gunpowder had been tried as early as 1680 by Christian Huygens, the Dutch physicist and astronomer, and Cayley himself had tried it in 1807. The explosive, however, had an obvious and unfortunate characteristic which led to a search for another solution. During the first half of the 19th century, experiments were undertaken with hot-air engines, it being reasoned that air, after all, was available everywhere and was safe. Unfortunately it was proven that an air engine, while it could be made to work, would have to be at least as large as a steam engine, thereby cancelling virtually all advantages it might have had.

A more positive step was taken in 1860 when Etienne Lenoire, working in France, produced the first even remotely practical internal combustion engine. It was practical only in the sense that it could be made to operate, but not in two other respects: it was far too large, and it consumed enormous quantities of illuminating gas as fuel. Though inefficient, it was nevertheless a beginning and development continued. Ironically the answer came from inventors who had no desire to become airborne.

"Horseless carriage" inventors shared some of the problems of the aviation enthusiasts: they needed an engine that was compact, self-contained and light and that could produce enough power to move their vehicles. By the 1880s success was at hand. Gottlieb Daimler and Carl Benz in Germany, working separately, each produced a successful automobile engine. By the end of the century many gasoline engines were being produced with the inevitable innovations and improvements. It wasn't long before the automobile engine took to the air.

By modifying a Pope-Toledo automobile engine, the Wrights solved the problem of powering an aircraft. Though far from efficient, or even from being as powerful as they could have made it, the engine was a starting point from which further experimentation could continue. Though the Wrights had proven an aircraft could be powered, a significant problem remained.

It was necessary to develop a means by which the power produced by an engine could be translated into thrust—motion. Though da Vinci and others had proved that a screw propeller was the answer, suprisingly little scientific research had been undertaken into the operation of propellers even by the first decade of the 20th century. Improvements in marine propellers, the area where these screws were most commonly used, occurred more as a result of trial and error than scientific investigation. Little was known about a propeller's operation, theoretically or otherwise, in the less dense medium. Orville Wright, in relating the problem involved in designing an air-screw, wrote:

> It is hard to find a point from which to make a start . . . for nothing about a propeller, or the medium in which it acts, stands still for a moment. The thrust depends upon the speed and the angle at which the blade strikes the air; the angle at which the air strikes the speed which the propeller is turning, the speed the machine is travelling forward, and the speed at which the air is travelling backward; the slip of the air backward depends upon the thrust exerted by the propeller and the amount of air acted upon. When any of these changes, it changes all the rest, so they are all interdependent upon one another. But these are only a few of the factors that must be considered.[7]

Once airborne, a whole new set of factors relating to control had to be considered. The Wrights were able to devise a system of controls that countered the various forces acting upon the aircraft, giving them the stability and safety they sought. Success was their's since they had correctly combined the several necessary yet independent elements.

The success of the Wrights and others with powered, fixed-wing aircraft prompted a number of helicopter enthusiasts to intensify their efforts, each wanting to be the first in his field. Surely, they thought, they must be at the threshold of success, but they were not as close as they hoped.

On August 24, 1907, a M. Volumard became the first man to be carried aloft in a helicopter. Designed and built by Louis and Charles Breguet, and Professor Richet at Roubaix, France, the machine resembled a St. Andrews (diagonal) cross in plan form. The V-8 engine, which could develop a maximum of 45 hp, was situated at the mid-point of the frame-work, above the "aeronaut's" seat and below the fuel tank. It drove four, four-bladed biplane rotors, one situated at the extremity of each leg. A contemporary account of the flight stated that "in the trials of the lifting power it was found that at the above speed of the planes (rotors, 48 rpm) the apparatus could rise in the air and keep itself off the ground at a height of a few feet."[8]

It was, however, apparently intended from the start that the machine would only test its lifting capacity because it could not be steered. Once it had succeeded in lifting and holding 1169 pounds in the air for one minute, the machine was deemed to have achieved its limits. It had flown—but just barely since it had been held down. Breguet then built another helicopter and flew it to a height of 15 feet on July 22, 1908, but it was wrecked. While Breguet had been busy with his experiments, another Frenchman had also achieved a degree of success.

Paul Cornu designed and built a twin-tandem rotor helicopter in 1908. Powered by a 24-hp Antoinette engine, a common aero engine of the period, the Cornu helicopter was neither restrained nor uncontrolled. A movable airfoil was situated at each end of the machine to permit it to climb or descend. Its only flight, which took place November 13, 1907 lasted a mere 20 seconds, but Cornu's helicopter was the first to fly without any attachment to the ground.

Experimentation with rotary-winged aircraft was not restricted to the West. In Russia, only two years after the first faltering flights of Breguet and Cornu, the son of a doctor began helicopter experiments. Igor Sikorsky, then a student, succeeded (if just barely) in getting an unmanned helicopter off the ground. Describing the helicopter years later, Sikorsky wrote that it

> had a wooden frame similar to a large rectangular box, with a 25 horsepower Anzani engine on one side and the proposed seat or platform for the operator on the other. In the centre of the frame was the transmission box. A large wooden pulley was connected by a four-inch-wide belt to a smaller pulley on the motor. Two concentric tubular shafts were connected with the transmission box and were guided by an upper bearing at the top of the frame. On each of the shafts there were mounted two three-bladed lifting propellers, the upper one having a diameter of about fifteen feet and the lower one sixteen and a half feet.[9]

The rotors turned in opposite directions, thus countering torque and dissymmetry of lift. The machine was not powerful enough to lift both itself and a pilot, and it vibrated fiercely. Despite the problems with this machine and a second one built a year later, which was also unsuccessful, Sikorsky was grateful for the information acquired since he now realized, at least in theory, what he was doing wrong. Though he did not lose interest in vertical-lift flight, Sikorsky came to the conclusion that it was wiser to concentrate on fixed-wing aircraft since technology was still too primitive to solve the problems inherent in designing a helicopter.

While the First World War brought with it tremendous advances in fixed-wing aircraft, including performance, increased size and better safety and reliability, no such claims could be made in the rotary-wing field. Not unreasonably, efforts and resources during wartime had to be expended on machines that had achieved a reasonable degree of refinement and for which military value could be demonstrated. The helicopter, at this stage, was simply not worthy of

intense development. Some experimentation did however continue.

A Danish pioneer, Jens Ellehammer, managed to get a twin coaxial-rotor helicopter of his design off the ground briefly in 1914. Like other helicopters of the period, it did not manage to get out of the ground effect. One helicopter that did climb clear of the ground cushion was produced for the Austrian Army in 1915. Lieutenant Stephan Petrozy designed and built a machine that he intended would be used for observation, but it was incapable of leaving the ground until redesigned by Professor von Karman. Though it could rise vertically to 150 feet it was unable to move in any direction but down from the hover. The only control feature was the ability to apply collective pitch, an equal angle of attack on all the rotor blades, to lift it into the air. In essence, nothing new had been developed.

Following the war, there was a renewed interest in helicopters. The April 1923 issue of *Scientific American* included an account of flights made by a United States Army-funded helicopter. In 1921 Georges de Bothezat, an ex-patriate Russian aeronautical engineer, managed to convince the US Government that he could produce a practical military helicopter. It took him two years to design and build a machine like the Breguet-Richet helicopter of 1907 in configuration. Powered by 170-hp LeRhone rotary engine, a type used extensively in military fixed-wing aircraft, the cruciform helicopter lifted 3600 pounds, including the weight of the pilot, fuel and aircraft.

It was claimed in the article that "the flight was steady and gave every assurance that the machine would perform at greater heights and would maintain remarkable stability in regular flight."[10] Directional control was achieved by means of small propellers, one for each manoeuvre. What would happen, the Army wondered, if one or more of the four main rotors quit? The resulting dissymmetry of lift would create serious problems for the pilot, rolling the cumbersome machine to the side where lift was lost. This potential difficulty and the complexity of the machine resulted in the cancellation of the project. De Bothezat, however, was undeterred and made other attempts to produce a workable helicopter for his ideas. Meanwhile other experimenters were working without government assistance.

It seems characteristic of helicopter pioneers that they had a high degree of perseverence. Like De Bothezat, the efforts of a father-and-son team of inventors, Emile and Henry Berliner, working in the United States, stretched over a period of two decades. Beginning in 1905, Berliner had built a machine which by 1909 had carried a man aloft a number of times. This was a significant achievement.

By September 1922 Henry had built and flown an aircraft based on his father's ideas. A contemporary account optimistically claimed that Berliner had "perfected the first successful helicopter which will rise perpendicularly from the ground, and when it has reached the desired elevation will fly ahead at whatever speed the operator desires."[11] It would fly ahead but still lacked the capability to manoeuvre in any other direction from the hover.

The fuselage resembled that of a contemporary fixed-wing aircraft, but there the resemblance ended.

Henri and Emile Berliner, working in the United States, produced this vertical-lift aircraft in 1922 after more than 20 years of experimentation. The contrarotating rotors on outriggers were powered by a single engine. Another horizontally mounted propeller situated behind the pilot on the fuselage decking controlled the attitude of the aircraft. (*Scientific American*)

Vertical ascent was achieved by means of two bilateral, fixed-pitch rotors, one on each side of the fuselage at the end of outriggers. Had a very tall pilot been employed, he might well have found himself abbreviated by the two-bladed rotors, which turned uncomfortably close to his head. Forward motion was achieved by tilting the whole aircraft in the direction desired. A horizontally-mounted propeller on the aft fuselage decking accomplished the evolution required. Lateral stability was assured by adjustable vanes situated below the rotors. While the aircraft flew, it was a clumsy solution to the problem and difficulties remained. The builder admitted that a descent from high altitude could be unsafe, and while it might be accomplished with skillful use of the throttle, another solution was needed.

The solution came as a result of the stall and crash of an airplane in Spain. Juan de la Cierva, a Spanish aeronautical engineer who had lost a friend in that crash, was determined to design an aircraft as near to being stall-proof as possible. If a fixed-wing stalled, lift would be lost and a crash was likely. The answer, it seemed to Cierva, was to provide a number of wings rotating about a central axis. Using models with a two-bladed rotor, he began a series of experiments. Each time the model rolled to one side—the direction in which the rotor turned. Gyroscopic action and dissymetry of lift made this inevitable.

Then came a breakthrough. Cierva made some fundamental changes in the rotor, so that his models, and ultimately his full-sized aircraft, flew without the lateral rolling motion. Long after the major problems had been worked out, he wrote a book, *Wings of Tomorrow: The Story of the Autogiro,* in which he explained the reason for his success.

... the essential secret of the Autogiro's successful flight is the characteristic flexibility as applied to its wings ... if the blades were free to move, the current of air induced by forward motion would adjust them automatically into the correct position for flight.[12]

The rotor of an autogiro was fully articulated; two hinges, one horizontal, the other vertical, attached the blades to the hub in a manner which allowed them full freedom of movement.

Few people at the time could understand how such a flexible and frail rotor could support a heavy aircraft. Cierva explained that "the explanation lies in a very familiar fact—the fact of centrifugal force. The disc created by the revolving rotor is actually a very strong and stable flying surface."[13] Each rotor blade flew into the air exactly in the same manner as a conventional airplane's wing—both require forward motion to fly. Forward motion was, as in an airplane, provided by a vertically mounted radial engine and propeller mounted in the nose. The rotor, which was always unpowered in flight, was in "autorotation;" that is to say, its blades had only a very slight positive angle of attack collectively and were turned by the flow of air coming from below while the aircraft moved forward. The means by which safe descents could be made had been discovered!

One problem with an autogiro, or to be more accurate, gyroplane, was that it could not become airborne until its rotor was turning at least 180 revolutions per minute. In order to accomplish this, several methods were employed: the first involved a rather lengthy take-off run which decreased the aircraft's short take-off capability to almost that of a conventional airplane; the second, which reduced the length of run, employed a pull cord to get the rotor turning—this was clearly inadequate. A third used the deflected prop wash, the air thrown back by the propeller, to turn the rotor; and in the fourth and most effective method, the rotor was connected to the engine by means of a shaft and clutch. The engine drive had to be declutched before flight was possible.

Another development which was later used in helicopters was the "swash plate." This device made possible the tilting of the rotor to achieve directional control on all four axes.

Throughout the 1920s and the 1930s the gyroplane underwent a number of improvements. Raoul Hafner, an Austrian working in Britain, designed a type with workable collective and cyclic controls, both of which were used in helicopters, by the mid-30s. These machines could take off at a steep angle —but not vertically. The autogiro and its equivalents could accomplish all that Cierva had hoped and more. The autogiro did not, however, even at its most sophisticated stage of development, have all the capabilities and features of a helicopter but it was never intended that it should. In spite of this, its success was a major advance towards a true helicopter. Interest in developing a true helicopter persisted, and large corporations became involved in the late 1920s.

In 1927 Maitland B. Bleeker, an engineer with the Curtiss Aeroplane and Motor Corporation in the United States, undertook helicopter research with the full backing of his employer. Three years later the result, a rather strange-looking machine, was proclaimed in *Scientific American* as having some promise of vertical flight. Power was provided by a standard Pratt and Whitney Wasp radial engine which was allowed to rotate, along with its oil and fuel tanks, above the fuselage on the mast. The rotor itself was turned by four small propellers, each mounted on the leading edge of a blade and driven by a complex system of shafts and gearing from the engine. This arrangement was intended to counter torque. Pitch control was accomplished by means of "Stabovators"—vanes—situated at and below the trailing edge of each rotor blade. This helicopter did fly after a fashion but proved so unstable and complex that further development was suspended.

In the early 1930s a Dutch scientist, Dr. A.G. von Baumhauer, produced a helicopter similar in configuration to a type produced by a Boris Yuriev in Russia in 1912—a single main rotor for lift and control, and a single anti-torque tail rotor. A small radial engine in the nose of Baumhauer's machine powered the main rotor via a long shaft, and a smaller engine in the tail drove an anti-torque rotor. This machine flew but later crashed, possibly as a result of control problems. It was another step towards the comparatively simple yet most effective configuration which would before long prove so successful.

In 1935 and 1936 Louis Breguet briefly re-established France's leadership in helicopter development with his third rotary-wing design. Along with his co-designer, René Dorand, he produced a twin coaxial-rotor helicopter which was able to capture several international records: height 518 feet, speed 27.32 mph, endurance 1 hr. 2 min. 50 sec.[14]

In 1935 Brough, in England, was the site for experiments by Dr. Oskar Asboth which produced positive results. The Blackburn Company well known for its naval aircraft, claimed that the Asboth machine could climb 1500 feet/minute and attain a forward speed of 100 mph. It, like the Breguet machine, was a coaxial type with the two rotors immediately behind the two-seat cabin adjacent to the machine's centre of gravity. Asboth had earlier built helicopters that attained heights of at least 50 feet on a hundred occasions. Lauren D. Lyman of the *New York Times,* who submitted the report, suggested that helicopters could be used for forest protection patrols and topographic survey.[15]

In Finland that same year, V. Louhia claimed he had invented a helicopter capable of 250 mph—an enviable if not visionary achievement. He claimed that it ran noiselessly without a propeller or wings and that it was able to carry great loads. If tests in England were to prove satisfactory, the inventor declared that it would soon be in production. Outlandish claims notwithstanding, progress was being made.

The German air force, the Luftwaffe, was rearming at this time in an environment that encouraged innovation. Professor E.H. Henrick Focke, in disfavour with the Nazi regime, left the Focke-Wulf company and soon began work independently on helicopter design. Focke, like a number of others, had gained experienced with rotary-wing designed by building autogiros under licence. The result of his own research, the Fa 61 of 1936, with its twin side-by-side rotors proved a great advance over earlier types. In 1937 the 160-hp Brandenburg engine carried the small aircraft to new records at Hoyken Kamp near Bremen: endurance 1 hr. 20 min. 49 sec., speed 77.6 mph, distance 50 miles.[16] The German machine aroused considerable interest and, in 1938, a paper prepared by Focke, together with films of the Fa 61, were a feature of a meeting of mechanical engineers in New York. The 1939 World's Fair in that city was to be the starting point for a transcontinental flight to San Francisco by a new 5-passenger helicopter by Focke-Achelis. It never took place.

The years just before and during the Second World War were critical to the development of the helicopter. Igor Sikorsky, who had cherished the idea of a

The first rotary-winged aircraft in British Columbia was this Pitcairn Autogiro photographed by Andy Duncan. An Ontario-based machine, it was in the Okanagan region with the Trans-Canada Air Tour of 1931, an event intended to increase public interest in aviation. (Andy Duncan Photo/ Okanagan Helicopters Collection)

direct lift aircraft since his first experiments in 1909, and had applied for a United States patent in 1931, was at last able to pursue serious studies with a view to actually producing a practical helicopter.

In the spring of 1939, Sikorsky was authorized to proceed with drawings for a helicopter.[17] United Aircraft Corporation, the parent company of Sikorsky Aircraft, was sufficiently impressed with the practicality of the project and, needless to say, with the engineering ability of Sikorsky to commit company resources to the development of a helicopter. In

148

view of the failure rate of others working towards the same end, it took courage to make this sort of commitment.

Having confidence in his own ideas, Sikorsky was undaunted by the high failure rate of others and went ahead with design and construction of what came to be called the VS300 (Vought-Sikorsky 300). By September 14, 1939, Sikorsky had completed the first version and was able to carry out a number of short hops; a remarkable achievement for less than six months' work.

The machine was purposely kept simple so that problems could be more easily isolated and corrected. The pilot sat in the open without protection of any kind. Development of the helicopter once again proved to be a process of constant revision. Severe vibration encountered in the first hops led to the rotational speed of the main rotor being reduced until the problem was corrected. By November 1939, hops of one or two minutes were possible. But the control problems that had plagued other experimenters still had to be ironed out. Various tail-rotor configurations were tried and new flying techniques developed. The latter were worked out using the helicopter without its rotors installed on a variable attitude test stand—a primitive simulator. It soon became obvious that in inexperienced hands the helicopter would easily roll to one side, so techniques were developed to counter this. Safety was soon improved enough that restraints were no longer necessary. By mid-summer 1940 both machine and techniques had developed to where Sikorsky was flying the helicopter for periods of 15 minutes under reasonably good control. Considering the difficulties, this was a milestone in the development of the helicopter. On May 6, 1941, the VS-300 established a world helicopter endurance record of just over 90 minutes.[18]

While Sikorsky was experimenting with the VS-300, others were attempting to turn their ideas into practical aircraft. Configurations other than the single tail rotor and single main rotor concept were tried with limited success. The first helicopter purchased for the US Army since that of DeBothezat in the 1920s closely resembled the German Fa 61 in form, with two contra-rotating rotors mounted on pylons extending at right angles to the fuselage, one on each side of the machine. The rotors were powered by an engine buried in the fuselage and were driven by long shafts carried out through the pylons. The designer, W. Laurence LePage, had had access to data gathered by the Germans with the Fa 61. In 1938 he and Havilland H. Platt, a mechanical engineer with similar ideas about helicopter development, formed a partnership to produced a rotary-winged craft. Congress, under the Dorsey Bill, provided ample incentive for ventures of this kind by voting $300,000 for the development of rotary-winged machines other than autogiros,[19] indicating that the US government thought a breakthrough in helicopters was imminent. Convinced that they had the answer, the Platt-LePage company began construction of a machine at their own expense before a contract had been awarded by the army. Their helicopter, which the army designated XR-1, flew by the summer of 1941, but control and perform-

There were a number of attempts to design and build a true helicopter in British Columbia during the 1930s and '40s. One of these was the Dubin helicopter. Equipped with contrarotating coaxial rotors to neutralize torque, this helicopter, like that produced by John Hess and sons in New Westminster a decade earlier, was unfortunately unsuccessful. Nick Dubin is on the left. (N. Dubin via Gordon Peters)

ance problems were such that development seemed unwarranted. The effect of Sikorsky's success by this time cannot be discounted.

Cut off from developments in the US by the war, the Germans continued research independently. Flettner succeeded in designing and manufacturing one of only two early helicopter types to see limited operational service. The F1282 Kolibri (Hummingbird) had two rotors side-by-side above the fuselage which were synchronized to pass between the blades of the other. Torque was countered by making the rotors contra-rotating; a tail rotor was rendered unnecessary as a consequence. This configuration worked well except on those rare occasions when there were synchronization problems. Then, rotor blades could shear off right down to the hub and the helicopter would crash. The idea of synchronized rotors was continued after the war by the Kaman company in the United States.

Meanwhile another helicopter was under development. The prototype, which ultimately proved as successful as Sikorsky's VS-300, took to the air at Gardenville, New York, in the summer of 1943. An engineer, Arthur Young, had developed his ideas for a two- rather than three-blade rotor. The Bell Model 30, an aircraft which was every bit as rudimentary as the VS-300, like the Sikorsky aircraft, initially showed an eagerness to roll over in inexperienced hands. Four large outriggers therefore were attached which imparted a greater degree of safety until tests solved control problems. The Model 30 was the progenitor of the successful Model 47 series, the first commercial model of which came onto the market in

1946. This machine was available in two configurations: the open cockpit 47-B3 for agricultural use and the fully enclosed 47-B for other operators. The former type was purchased by Okanagan Air Services in 1947 for use in British Columbia. Bell took the course over succeeding years of progressively developing the basic Model 47. Meanwhile other manufacturers whose machines would be used in British Columbia were also hard at work giving substance to their ideas.

While these first successful machines were still somewhat primitive, the major problems had been solved. A "watershed" in the technology had been reached and improvements to existing helicopters and new designs came quickly. Stanley Hiller, who would go on to produce the versatile and successful Hiller 12E helicopter, had begun experiments with rotary-wing craft at the age of 19 in 1944. He designed and built two coaxial-rotor machines before settling on the single main and tail-rotor configuration. The Hiller 360, similar to the 12E, was awarded its certificate of airworthiness on October 14, 1948.

There had always been helicopter designers interested in twin-rotor configurations—coaxial, intermeshing and side-by-side—but few tandem twin-rotor types had received attention. Undoubtedly the problems in developing a suitable power train had contributed to this. Frank N. Piasecki perfected this latter type and went on to produce designs such as the Vertol H-21A, in which tandem rotors were driven by a single engine. These helicopters came to be widely used in search and rescue, medium-lift transport and airline service. The Piasecki company was taken over by Vertol and eventually became Boeing-Vertol.

While the basic problems had been solved by the early 1950s, most helicopters were still limited in payload and performance. Manufacturers, naturally enough, took steps to improve their product. With the Korean War, there was considerable incentive. An automatic pilot was developed using a Sikorsky S-51 (H-5), and a self-contained navigational system was produced for the S-58. Though neither of these features would have much impact in British Columbia, where short-distance flights were the rule, other developments, such as the pitch, yaw and roll control system used in the Sikorsky S-55, would prove useful. Helicopters were becoming more sophisticated.

The introduction of turbines to helicopters in the mid-1950s greatly enhanced their versatility and capacity once some of the teething troubles were worked out. Another advantage of turbines was that they were smaller. They could free more space in the aircraft for passengers for internally stowed cargo. Other innovations, such as skids to replace castoring landing gears, bear paws, better cargo hooks and slings, when combined with innovative flying techniques, have made helicopters the most versatile aircraft in use today and a worthy fulfilment of the dreams of the ancients.

Sikorsky's VS-300 was, in its initial form, quite rudimentary. One advantage of this approach was that new ideas could be tried and accepted or discarded readily. Parts such as tail rotors could be added and kept if they worked, or cut off and replaced if they didn't. (United Technologies/ Sikorsky Aircraft)

## Notes

1. Ivor B. Hart, *The World of Leonardo da Vinci: Man of Science, Engineer and Dreamer of Flight.* London, MacDonald, 1961, p. 328.
2. Charles Gablehouse, *Helicopters and Autogiros: A History of Rotary Wing and V/STOL Aviation.* Philadelphia, J.B. Lippincott, 1969, p. 3.
3. J. Lawrence Pritchard, *Sir George Cayley: The Inventor of the Airplane.* London, Max Parrish, 1961, p. 197.
4. *Ibid.,* p. 227.
5. Svante Stubelius, *Balloon, Flying Machine, Helicopter: Further Studies in the History of Terms for Aircraft in English.* Göteborg, Göteborg Universitets, Arss Krift, vol. LXVI, 1960, p. 256.
6. "A New Aerial Machine," *Scientific American,* vol. LII, no. 19, May 9, 1885, p. 291.
7. John Evangelist Walsh, *One Day at Kitty Hawk: The Untold Story of the Wright Brothers and the Airplane.* New York, Thomas A. Crowell, 1975, p. 114.
8. "The Breguet Gyroplane," *Scientific American,* vol. 92 no. 20, November 16, 1907, p. 354.
9. Igor I. Sikorsky, *The Story of the Winged "S": An Autobiography.* New York, Dodd, Mead & Co., 1967, p. 25.
10. "Our Army's Helicopter," *Scientific American,* vol. 128 no. 4, April 4, 1923, p. 243.
11. "A Helicopter that Flies: The Berliner Machine," *Scientific American,* vol. 127 no. 3, September 1922, p. 160.
12. Juan de la Cierva and Don Rose, ed., *Wings of Tomorrow: The Story of the Autogiro.* New York, Brewer, Warren and Putnam, 1931, p. 91.
13. *Ibid.,* p. 115.
14. "Along the Far Flung Airways: New Helicopter Establishes World Records in Germany." *New York Times,* August 1, 1937, XI, p. 6.
15. Lauren D. Lyman, "Helicopter Again Tried: British Are Building One Expected to Have a Range of Two Hours." *New York Times,* March 24, 1935, VIII, 17-1.
16. "Professor H. Focke Claims World's Altitude, Distance and Speed Records: Bremen, Germany." *New York Times,* July 4, 1937, 3:3.
17. In British Columbia too, there were attempts to develop a helicopter. A John Hess and Sons were hard at work. After fifteen years of exhaustive tests and exptenditure of $30,000 they felt that they were near success. They had, by July 1936, taken out patents for a four-rotor craft in 42 countries. Plans were a closely-guarded secret. It was not successful.
"New Westminster Man Perfects Helicopter," *Vancouver Sun,* July 15, 1936, p. 3.
18. Sikorsky, *op. cit.,* p. 217.
19. H. Franklin Gregory, *The Helicopter.* Cranbury, New Jersey, A.S. Barnes, 1976, p. 64.

# Helicopter Types Used in British Columbia

## Aerospatiale
SA 318C Alouette Astazou,
SA 316B Alouette III Astazou,
SA 341G Gazelle,
SA 350B Astar,
SA 350D Astar,

## Bell
204B
205 A-1 (CH-118 in Canadian Forces)
206A, 206B (CH-136, CH-139 in
  Canadian Forces)
206L
212 (CH-135 in Canadian Forces)
214B
412
Bell 47 series (for details, see below)

## Boeing-Vertol
107-II (CH-113, CH-113A in
  Canadian Forces)

## Brantley
B2A
305

## Fairchild Hiller
FH 1100

## Hiller
12E (CH-112 in Canadian Army)

## Hughes
300
500
500C
500D

## Robinson
R22

## Sikorsky
S-51 (H-5 in RCAF, HO3S in USCG)
S-55 (H-19 in RCAF, HO4S in USCG)
S-55T
S-58B (H-34 in RCAF)
S-58T
S-61L
S-61N
S-62A (HH-52A in USCG)
S-64E
S-76

## Vertol
42
44
H-21A

# Bell 47 versions used in British Columbia

## Bell 47-B3
*Type*  2-seat light utility
*Engine*  178-hp Franklin 6V4
  6-cylinder horizontally-opposed,
  fan assisted, air-cooled

**Dimensions**
*Rotor dia.*  35 ft 1½ in
*Length*  27 ft 4 in
*Height*  9 ft 2 in

**Performance**
*Cruise speed*  92 mph
*Max. climb*  900 ft/min
*Service ceiling*  11,500 ft
*Hovering ceiling in ground effect*
  5400 ft
*Range*  212 miles

The Bell 47-B3 was a 2-seat, open-cockpit machine intended primarily for agricultural industry; two dust bins were provided, one on each side, and a dust-dispersing mechanism. The first delivery of a 47-B3 was made on December 31, 1946 and this was the first type of helicopter purchased for use in British Columbia.

## Bell 47-D and D1
*Type*  3-seat utility
*Engine*  178-hp (47-D) or 200-hp
  (47-D1) Franklin 6V4

**Dimensions**
*Rotor dia.*  35 ft 1½ in
*Length*  27 ft 4 in
*Height*  9 ft 2 in

**Performance**
*Cruise speed*  92 mph
*Max. climb*  900 ft/min
*Service ceiling*  11,500 ft
*Hovering ceiling in ground effect*
  5400 ft
*Range*  212 miles

Incorporated several changes over earlier models, being first with characteristic bubble cockpit enclosure. Fuel tank mounted transversely behind mast and above fuselage. It had been enclosed and mounted below engine on earlier models. Tail boom stripped to decrease weight and a fin added below boom and ahead of "harp" or rotor guard to increase longtitudinal stability. Cockpit enlarged to provide extra seat.

## Bell 47-G
Specifications as for 47-D1, except that range increased. Two saddle tanks, one one either side of main rotor mast, replaced single transverse tank on D1.

## Bell 47-G2
Dimensions as for 47-G; performance improved by substitution of Lycoming VO-435, 260-hp engine, de-rated to 220-hp because of transmission limitations (VO designates Vertical Opposed; TVO, Turbocharged Vertical Opposed).

## Bell 47-G2A
Dimensions as for 47-G2, except the main rotor blades were enlarged and tail boom lengthened. Engine: 240-hp Lycoming VO 435, with wet-sump lubrication system.

## Bell 47-G3
Dimensions as for the 47-G2, except main rotor blade size increased and tail boom lengthened. Performance, particularly at altitude, substantially improved with 240-hp Franklin 6V4-335A engine (turbocharged but with no governor to control the waste-gate); hence very easy to damage engine by "over-boosting" it).

## Bell 47-G3B
Specifications as for 47-G3, except engine was 260-hp turbocharged Lycoming TVO-435.

## Bell 47-G3B-1
*Type*  3-seat general purpose
*Engine*  270-hp Lycoming TVO-435

**Dimensions**
*Rotor dia.*  37 ft 1½ in
*Length*  31 ft 7 in
*Height*  9 ft 3__¾ in

**Performance**
*Cruise speed*  84 mph
*Max. inclined climb*  880 ft/min
*Hovering ceiling in ground effect*
  16,100 ft
*Service ceiling*  19,000 ft
*Range at 6000 ft*  247 miles
*External sling capacity*  1000 lb

Larger fuel tanks; wider cockpit; longer and heavier main rotor blades.

## Bell 47-G3B-2

Engine used was 280-hp Lycoming TVO-435. 900 series transmission fitted to accommodate increased power. Instrument pedestal in cockpit shortened to allow better forward visibility.

## Bell 47-G3B-2A

As above, except that Lycoming engine was equipped with wet-sump lubrication system.

## Bell 47-G4

Specifications as for the 47-G3B-1, except engine was Lycoming VO-540 of 315-hp, de-rated to 260-hp, and fitted with Bell-designed tuned crankshaft to avoid problems caused by 3-harmonic vibration in 540 engine of Hiller 12E.

## Bell 47-G4A

As above, with a 270-hp Lycoming VO-540 engine and 900 series transmission.

## Bell 47-G5

Agricultural spray version of 47-G4, except engine was Lycoming VO-435

Bell 47-G series was development of 47-D using variety of engines and detail improvements such as optional use of metal blades. Production of Bell model 47-G2 series began in 1953; finished in 1974. Model 47G-3B-2A and 47G-5A were final Bell 47s produced. Bell 47 historically the most widely-used piston helicopter in British Columbia.

## Bell 47-H

*Type* 3-seat general purpose
*Engine* 200-hp Franklin 6V4 6-cylinder air-cooled

**Dimensions**
*Rotor dia.* 35 ft 1½ in
*Length* 27 ft 4 in
*Height* 9 ft 3 in

**Performance**
*Max. cruise speed* 94 mph
*Max. inclined climb* 830 ft/min
*Hovering ceiling in ground effect* 9900 ft
*Range* 219 miles

Similar to the 47-G series but with an enclosed fuselage. Used by Helicopter Division of Pacific Western Airlines in British Columbia. First announced in 1954.

## Bell 47-J, 47-J2 and 47-J2A

*Type* 4-seat general purpose
*Engine* 220-hp Lycoming VO-435 (47-J) or 260-hp Lycoming VO-540 (47-J2)

**Dimensions**
*Rotor dia.* 37 ft
*Length* 32 ft 4¾ in
*Height* 9 ft 3½ in

**Performance**
*Max. speed* 105 mph
*Inclined climb* 870 ft/min
*Hovering ceiling in ground effect* 8400 ft
*Service ceiling* 11,000 ft
*Range* 285 miles

Commercial deliveries began in 1956. Most recent version in British Columbia is turbocharged 47-J2A. Designed for "executive" use with pilot in single seat in front of bubble and passengers on a bench seat behind.

## The Soloy Conversion

By 1970s performance of turbine helicopters superior to that of piston-engined Bell 47 and Hiller 12E, so attempt made to upgrade these by conversion to turbines. This process, which in effect recycled old aircraft, less costly than purchasing all-new turbine machines.

Joe Soloy of Chehalis, Washington, former Alaska helicopter pilot, headed firm which developed and manufactured conversion kit for use in British Columbia. Vancouver Island Helicopters of Victoria, first in Canada to acquire the kits and one of the earliest anywhere, converted all but one of its Bell 47s to turbines. Alf Stringer praised the kit for its quality; all components fitted precisely, and after conversion helicopters flew more smoothly.

**Specifications**
*Engine* 420-shp Allison 250-C20B

**Performance**
*Max. climb* 1250 ft/min
*Max. vertical climb* 970 ft/min
*Max. cruise* 95 mph

Upon conversion, all models of helicopter standardized with new plug electrical system, low profile instrument panel, weighted-tip main rotor blades, heavy-duty hub bearings, late-style tail rotor system, -123 engine mount assembly, auxiliary fuel pump installed, hydraulically-boosted collective controls, and smaller oil cooler on 47 G-4/G-4A

# Bibliography

## Books

Berget, Alphonse. *The Conquest of the Air.* London, William Heineman, 1911.

Cierva, Juan de la and Rose, Don, ed. *Wings of Tomorrow: The Story of the Autogiro.* New York, Brewer, Warren and Putnam, 1931.

Fay, John. *The Helicopter: History, Piloting, and How it Flies.* Newton Abbot, David and Charles, 1978.

Gablehouse, Charles. *Helicopters and Autogiros: A History of Rotating Wing and V/STOL Aviation.* Philadelphia, J.B. Lippincott, 1969.

Green, William and Pollinger, Gerald. *The Aircraft of the World.* London, Macdonald, 1965.

Gregory, H. Franklin. *The Helicopter: A Pictorial History.* Cranbury, N.J., A.S. Barnes, 1976

Hart, Ivor B. *The World of Leonardo da Vinci: Man of Science, Engineer, and Dreamer of Flight.* London, Macdonald, 1961.

Hubler, Richard G. *Straight Up: The Story of Vertical Flight.* New York, Duell, Sloan and Pierce, 1961.

Kaplan, H.R. and Hunt, James F. *This Is the Coast Guard.* Cambridge, Maryland, Cornell Maritime Press, 1972.

Milberry, Larry. *Aviation in Canada.* Toronto, McGraw-Hill Ryerson, 1979.

Moolman, Valerie. *The Road to Kittyhawk.* Alexandria, Time-Life, 1980.

Pritchard, J. Laurence. *Sir George Cayley: The Inventor of the Airplane.* London, Max Parrish, 1961.

Sikorsky, Igor I. *The Story of the Winged "S": An Autobiography.* New York, Dodd, Mead & Co., 1967.

Stubelius, Svante. *Balloon, Flying Machine, Helicopter: Further Studies in the History of Terms for Aircraft in English.* Göteborg, Göteborgs Universitets, Arss Krift vol. LXVI, 1960.

Taylor, Michael J.F., comp. and Taylor, John W.R., ed. *Jane's Pocket Book of Helicopters.* New York, Collier, 1981.

Turner, Charles C. *Aerial Navigation of Today: A Popular Account of the Evolution of Aeronautics.* Philadelphia, J.B. Lippincott, 1910.

Walsh, John Evangelist. *One Day at Kittyhawk: The Untold Story of the Wright Brothers and the Airplane.* New York, Thomas Y. Crowell, 1975.

Young, Arthur M. *The Bell Notes: A Journey from Physics to Metaphysics.* N.Y., Delacourt Press, 1979.

## Booklet

Dietrich Collins Equipment. *The Alcan Story.* Vancouver, F.W. Lees, N.D.

## Reference sources

"The Bell 212 Twin: It Makes Every Plane in Your Fleet More Effective." Fort Worth, Bell Helicopter, 1975, 18 pages.

"Construction . . . By Air." Stratford, Sikorsky Divison of United Aircraft, June 1958, 18 pages.

"S-62: First Turbine Powered Helicopter with Built-in Amphibious Capabilities." Stratford, Sikorsky Division of United Aircraft, n.d., 24 pages.

"The S-76." Stratford, Sikorsky Aircraft: United Technologies, September 1981, 32 pages.

*Air Search and Rescue: 63 Years of Aerial Lifesaving, A Pictorial History 1915-1978.* Alexandria, V.A., Department of Transportation, Coast Guard, 1978.

## Articles—Signed

Diamond, Gordon, Cliff Fletcher, and Hal Morrison. "S.O.S." *Prinsendam!* Rescue on the High Seas." *Sentinel,* vol. 16 no. 5, pp. 16-17.

Edwards, Les., "Okanagan Helicopters." *Air World,* March/April 1967, pp. 128-130.

Emerson, G.C. "Topographical Mapping by Helicopter." *Canadian Surveyor,* vol. X, no. 11, January 1952, pp. 3-11.

Graf, Cherry. "Heavy Lift Division Logs." *Rotortales,* vol. 2, no. 4, August 1981, pp. 1–3.

Foly, Dennis C. "Ode to the R4." *CAHS Journal,* vol. 18, no. 4, Winter 1980, pp. 112–115, 124.

Hanson, Phil. "West Coast Helilogging: Reaping the Harvest with Rotary Wings." *Canadian Aviation,* vol. 52, no. 8, August 1979, pp. 21-24.

Keith, Ronald A. "Okanagan Helicopters: World Wide Operations with 161 Whirly-birds." *Exxon Air World,* vol. 32, no. 2, 1980, pp. 26-29.

Keith, Ronald A. "The Versatility of Conair." *Canadian Aviation,* vol. 54, no. 3, March 1981, pp. 22-25.

Klemin, Alexander. "Sikorsky's Helicopter." *Scientific American,* vol. 163, no. 1, October 1940, pp. 189.

Morgan, David G. "B.C.'s Rapattack." *Canadian Aviation,* vol. 54, no. 7, July 1981, p. 39.

Randell, Keith. "Banner Year in '79 Prompts High Hopes for '80's." *Canadian Aviation,* vol. 53, no. 1, January 1980, pp. 20-24.

Sims, Donald. "Out of a Lifeboat into the Air." *Air International,* vol. 13, no. 4, October 1977, pp. 190-196.

Torney, Ralph. "Logging by Helicopter in B.C.: An Overview." *Canadian Forest Industries,* vol. 120, no. 3, March 1980, pp. 14-16.

Tower, Courtney. "Too Busy to Fly." *Canadian Aviation,* vol. 30, no. 1, January 1957, p. 56.

Wall, Rick. ''Between a Rock and a Cold Place.''
*Approach,* vol. 27, no. 8, February 1982, pp. 2-6.
Wenzel, Jan Udo. ''Skyhook.'' *Western Wings,*
vol. 4, June 1959, pp. 5-6.
Woodcock, Don. ''The Prinsendam Recue: An
Account of the Greatest Marine Rescue of Modern
Times.'' *Westworld,* vol. 7, no. 7, November 1981,
pp. 21-23.

## Articles—Unsigned
''The Breguet Gyroplane.'' *Scientific American,* vol.
92, no. 20, November 16, 1907, p. 354.
''Driptorch: A New Technique Helps Slash Burning
Problem.'' *Timberline,* vol. 4, no. 7, October 1976,
pp. 4-5.
''A Helicopter That Flies—The Berliner Machine.''
*Scientific American,* vol. 127, no. 3, September
1922, p. 160.
''The Helicopter Triumphant.'' *Scientific American,*
vol. 161, no. 1, January 1939, p. 30.
''A New Aerial Machine.'' *Scientific American,*
vol. LII, no. 19, May 9, 1885, p. 291.
''Presentation of Awards.'' *Newsletter:* Canadian
Coast Guard, Victoria, vol. 2, no. 17, May 1976,
pp. 2-4.
''Rotary Wings Among the Mountains: The Story of
Okanagan Helicopters Ltd.'' *Esso Air World,* Nov/
Dec 1952, 4 pages.
''Trees from the Sky.'' *Harmac News,* December
1951, pp. 12-13.

## Interviews
Art Johnson   January 15, 1981
Ernie McMinn   February 5, 1981
Bruce Payne   February 25, 1981
Alf Stringer   April 1, 1981
Eric Cowden   May 15, 1981
Ian Duncan   May 29, 1981
Bob Jones   June 9, 1981
Lynn Stringer   June 26, 1981
Bill McLeod   June 29, 1981
Ivor Roberts   July 28, 1981
Barney Bent   August 10, 1981
Joan McLeod   September 8, 1981
Ken Blackwood and Don Mackenzie
   October 15, 1981
Will Tompson   October 30, 1981
Jock Graham   December 3, 1981
Bob Taylor   March 14, 1982
Mrs. Anne Agar and Mrs. Ada Carlson
   March 16, 1982
Lt.-Col. C.G. Diamond, CD, CAF, April 27, 1982
Walter Palubiski   May 1982
Hugh Lyons   June 3, 1982
Commander Paul Milligan, USCG, Ltd. Commander
   Dennis Maclean, USCG, and Ensign Jeff Vail, USCG
   June 16, 1982

# Index